Acclaim for Julie Hecht's

WAS THIS MAN A GENIUS?

"A revelation. . . . The journey here is as rewarding as the destination."   —*Newsday*

"In the seventies, the author repeatedly attempted to interview the late Andy Kaufman, and fell prey to the confusion of life and art that marked his peculiar talent. Here Hecht returns the favor: in this account of her comic ordeal, she has created for her eccentric subject a final act."   —*The New Yorker*

"Hecht quietly reveals herself as the perfect foil to Kaufman's antics: centered, skeptical . . . but not without humor or compassion."   —*Kirkus Reviews*

"Entertaining hours in the presence of the life and mind of a uniquely gifted and exasperating individual, and the singular world he managed to create for himself, and . . . for us."   —*Rocky Mountain News*

Julie Hecht

Was This Man a Genius?

Julie Hecht was born in Manhattan. She is
the author of *Do the Windows Open?*, a
collection of stories, all of which appeared in
The New Yorker. Other stories have also been
published in *Harper's* and *The New Yorker*,
and she has won an O. Henry Prize. In 1998
she was awarded a Guggenheim Fellowship.
She lives on the east end of Long Island
in the winter and in Massachusetts in the
summer.

ALSO BY JULIE HECHT

Do the Windows Open?

WAS THIS MAN A GENIUS?

Was This Man a Genius?

TALKS WITH ANDY KAUFMAN

Julie Hecht

VINTAGE BOOKS

A DIVISION OF RANDOM HOUSE, INC.

NEW YORK

FIRST VINTAGE BOOKS EDITION, JULY 2002

The Library of Congress has cataloged the Random House edition as
follows:
Hecht, Julie.
Was this man a genius? : talks with Andy Kaufman / Julie Hecht.—1st ed.
p. cm.
ISBN 0-375-50457-5 (alk. paper)
1. Kaufman, Andy, 1949–1984—Anecdotes. I. Title.
PN2287.K28 H43 2001
792.7'028'092—dc21 00-062720

Vintage ISBN: 0-375-72520-2

www.vintagebooks.com

Printed in the United States of America
10 9 8 7 6 5 4 3 2 1

FOR ANDY KAUFMAN

Introduction

In the winter of 1978, I was invited to a lunch for contributors to *Harper's Magazine*. I believed that short stories were valued by society and that was the reason for the invitation. However, at the time, as is still the case, writers of short stories were regarded with suspicion. During the lunch, Lewis Lapham, the editor, suggested that I write a "piece" on this or that for "us." I didn't like the words *piece for us*, and I reminded Lewis that I wrote short stories.

"Isn't there anything you really want to find out about, and write about?" he asked me. I explained a few times, in different ways, that I wasn't a journalist. I watched Tom Wolfe eat his lobster bisque. He had excellent table manners. Then I walked back home. I was thinking dark thoughts.

Around that time I read that Andy Kaufman would be performing at Town Hall. I had seen him sing "Pop Goes the Weasel" when he appeared as a special guest on *Saturday Night Live*, and one thing I did want to find out was how Andy Kaufman had gotten to do what he was doing. I especially wanted to know how he came to sing that song the way he did. I got the idea that I would meet him, talk to him, find out the answer, and I would write about it. I asked my editor at *Harper's* whether she'd like to go see him perform at Town Hall. She said yes.

I spent a year meeting Andy whenever he came to New York to perform. The meetings consisted of hanging out wherever he was and taping whatever happened, but he wouldn't tell me what I wanted to know until the end of the year. The 150-page manuscript turned out to be too long for *Harper's* and the story was considered to be too strange to be published. When I told Andy about all this, he said, "Don't worry about it. The story is ahead of its time, the way I'm ahead of my time."

Most people didn't know who Andy was. He had made a special for a television network, but no network would show it.

"They won't show my special and now they won't publish your story," Andy said. "We're in the same boat."

"I'm in a worse boat," I said.

"No, it's the same boat exactly," Andy said.

ONE NIGHT about a year later, I was sitting on the couch watching the ten o'clock news when Andy called. "Why don't you ever call me anymore?" he said.

"Well, I finished my story. I don't have any more questions."

"But aren't we still friends?" Andy asked.

"You said you were too busy to have any more friends," I said.

"But then we did the story together. We both worked at it."

"For me it was work, for you it was play," I said.

"And wasn't that fun, work and play, the combination?" Andy said.

"Yes, but the story is in a carton. I thought the grounds for friendship might be gone," I said.

"You should never think that. People work and work on things and this happens. That's show business. You have to get used to it."

"But I'm not in show business," I said.

"Oh. That's right," Andy said. "You should get used to it anyway. We'll always be friends, right?"

That was that for twenty years.

. . .

AFTER ANDY'S work was rediscovered, various people kept asking, "What about that Andy Kaufman thing you did?" This gave me the idea to rewrite and edit the story in order to show some true part of Andy Kaufman's life the way he talked about it.

WAS THIS MAN A GENIUS?

NOT FUNNY

"I JUST WANT THE audience to have a wonderful, happy feeling inside them and leave with big smiles on their faces," Andy told me with a blank stare the first time I met him. "I can't help it if people laugh, I'm not trying to be funny," he explained. He said that he felt insulted when he saw reviews calling him a comedian. "I wouldn't mind being compared to Charlie Chaplin or W. C. Fields," he said sadly. "But I don't find most comedy funny."

People were surprised when they heard Andy speak on TV for the first time. He spoke with a foreign accent, but it was impossible to be sure what kind of accent it was, because it sounded in between Pakistani and Jamaican. Someone with the name "Andy Kaufman" was probably from New York, not Pakistan, and this made the accent even more mysterious.

"No one else would have me when I got put on *Saturday Night Live* in 1975," Andy told me when I met him. After the first show, when the cast appeared to wave good-bye, Andy wasn't there. The time he did come out, at the end of one of the later shows, he stood by himself and stared into the camera. He wore a gray hooded sweatshirt with the hood on his head.

"I wasn't trying to be funny," he said when I asked about the the sweatshirt. "I was dressed to leave and they said to come out onstage for the good-byes, so I did. This is what I really wear outside. I can't help it if people think it's funny."

It hadn't been easy to get to talk to Andy for the first time. "What's it for, some kinda movie magazine or what?" Andy's manager, George Shapiro, asked me over the phone from Beverly Hills. I explained what, but George wasn't impressed. "Yeah, well, Andy doesn't like to do these things, and he's gonna be very busy when he's in New York for Town Hall. But, listen, he's also gonna perform the same week at his high school, in Great Neck, and this is a great triumph for him, because he was so shy in high school. You can go out there and talk to him for a few minutes after the concert." I realized that a number of people in Beverly Hills spoke with New York accents.

· · ·

ANDY'S MOTHER, on the phone from her home in Great Neck, sounded surprised to hear that her son was a genius. She laughed when I said the word. I asked her whether Andy's father was Stanley Kauffman the film critic, and she said no, he was Stanley Kaufman of the costume-jewelry business and that she was a homemaker and mother. Andy had a younger brother, Michael, and a younger sister, Carol. They both were students and weren't in show business. If Andy was from a regular family, the question of how he got to be the way he was seemed even more mysterious. I wanted to come right out and ask his mother, but it was too soon for that.

Andy himself, on the phone from Los Angeles, said he was rushing out to perform at the Comedy Store. Every few minutes, he'd say, "I'm late, I haven't meditated yet, I don't have time for this." When he called back after his performance, he had a list of questions: "How tall are you? When is your birthday? What color hair do you have? I just want to know whether I'd be interested in having a love affair with you. You could get me to give away all my secrets and then you could use them in your story."

"Couldn't you tell the secrets any other way?"

"Yeah, probably, but with my pants up I'd give away less than with my pants down."

"Maybe this wasn't such a good idea," I said.

"I'm just kidding," Andy said. "But wouldn't it be great if you were my dream girl, a girl from my fantasies?"

THE NEXT time I heard from Andy he was at the airport in New York. "I just got in from L.A.," Andy said. "On the plane, I realized from our conversations that you're married. I wasted all my fantasies on you. I thought I'd found my dream girl, a writer who looks like Goldie Hawn and lives alone in the heart of Greenwich Village."

"The Goldie Hawn part was your idea," I said.

"It's true. I'm hoping that everyone I meet will look like her, and when I'm in New York I have to get all the girls I can."

"Couldn't you allot a small amount of time to this story and then return to that?"

"Well, I don't have much time. I'm very busy. And whatever spare time I have, I try to get girls. That's what I say every time I'm here, but usually it doesn't work and I end up alone in my hotel room."

"Then what?"

"Oh, watch television, make phone calls, eat dinner, and go to sleep."

"Has getting girls always been the most important thing on your schedule?"

"Yes. Well, no. I never had any girls until recently. I

never had a girlfriend in high school or college, so now I want to make up for it. I was too shy before. But now girls come up to me and they know who I am. They volunteer themselves to me."

"Don't you do enough of this kind of thing in California?"

"I *try*, I'm always *trying*. But I live there now, so now when I come to New York it's like a vacation, and getting girls is how I want to spend my time. I'm not successful in California—here either—but wherever I go, I try. Mostly I fail, but I hope, in time, to improve and have all the girls I want. I hope to get the knack of it."

I KNEW that Great Neck was the kind of suburb I wanted to avoid. I tried thinking about it as if I were a reviewer who had to review the concert, and that way I wouldn't be going to Great Neck itself but only to the concert. When I got to the high school, I saw that there were no real reviewers in the audience—they all knew how to get tickets from Andy's manager for his Town Hall performance. In my case, I'd been told to call a lot of different promoters and agents, who all told me to call the other ones.

GREAT NECK

ONCE INSIDE THE Great Neck High School auditorium, I was given fine treatment; a student showed me
to four seats reserved for me and my party, although I was
the only one in my party willing to go to Great Neck. Kids
in the auditorium were not like kids I remembered in au-
ditoriums of the sixties. This was an unruly bunch, looking wild and making a lot of noise. They seemed to be in
control of the place.

It was easy to spot Andy's parents amidst this crew.
They were neatly dressed in the kind of clothes people
wore in suburbs—turtleneck sweaters, pleated slacks, and
jackets with lapels. Mrs. Kaufman didn't look like the
mother of a twenty-eight-year-old man, especially a man
like Andy. I looked at Andy's father and mother and won-

dered how these parents had ever come up with a son like that.

When I met Mrs. Kaufman, I told her how much I loved Andy's work and that I had been his fan ever since I'd seen him perform as a guest on *Saturday Night Live*.

"Where's your husband tonight?" she asked in a threatening way.

"He's working, but he loves Andy, too, and he wanted to come to the concert."

"Doesn't he mind your coming here alone without him?"

"I mean, I love Andy as a performer. This is my work."

"These kids nowadays," said one of her friends who was sitting nearby and listening. "That's the way they think."

When the concert didn't begin on time, the mob of high school students began screaming for Andy. I was glad to see that this many people knew who he was and appreciated him. Soon Andy danced onto the stage holding a microphone and singing "Oklahoma." He skipped around as if he had springs in his legs, and he sang in an unprofessional voice. He sounded like a boy who was singing just for fun. The sight of the springy skipping around with the sound of that voice seemed to be what made the audience laugh. When he finished singing, he began to speak with the unrecognizable foreign accent. The foreign man started to tell some jokes in a meek and nervous way, and when the audience didn't laugh, he began to laugh himself. It was a nervous laugh on the way to hysteria. Then the audience began to boo and the foreign man started to apologize. Somehow during the apology he began to cry. He was talking, apologizing, and cyring all at the same time, and the audience was laughing. When he recovered, he said he'd like to do some imitations, but they weren't exactly imitations, since there was no resemblance to the people being imitated. The audience kept laughing. Finally, he said, "Now I would like to do de Elvis Presley." He turned around to an old suitcase on a chair and changed into a costume—or half a costume, a homemade-looking invention that started with the same white bell-bottom pants he'd had on. He ripped off some tape on the outside seam of each leg to show spangles and then took a satin-looking glitter-covered jacket and put it on over his black turtleneck sweater.

He picked up a guitar from a chair behind him, turned back around to face the audience with Elvis Presley's expression on his face, and did a perfect imitation of Elvis Presley singing. Somehow the foreign man now had Elvis

Presley's voice. The audience of kids went crazy with happiness. When he finished singing, Andy stepped forward and, in the foreign accent again, said, "Tenk you vedy much." The screaming and applause was the kind I'd seen in a film about the Rolling Stones.

"I'm not trying to be funny," Andy told me later. "I just thought that 'Oklahoma' would be a good opening song. I don't know why it's funny. If you keep asking me these stupid questions, I'll get mad and I won't talk to you anymore. I'm just singing a song, and if people want to laugh that's their business."

When I asked how he'd learned to do such a great imitation of Elvis, he said, "All my life I listened to his records and practiced in my room."

After the concert was over, I waited outside Andy's dressing room for the planned time to talk to him. Waiting with me were some of the wild-looking kids and a few others, who looked as if they were hoping to go to Harvard in the future. Andy's father came over and sat down. "Andy was the first in our neighborhood to entertain at children's birthday parties," he told me. "Lily Tomlin heckled him in Los Angeles, but then she apologized and explained she thought he was a real artist."

"He's as talented as she is," I said.

"Well, I don't know about *that*," Andy's father said.

A guy named Bob came along and said he was Andy's road manager. I believed him, because he had long blond hair and was wearing a cap with a visor. Bob told me what he did, and immediately got me to believe that he was just a guy who hung out with Andy and helped him with his concerts.

"The first time I saw Andy talk in his normal voice to Johnny Carson, I figured that he was a normal boy and that he came from a regular family from Brooklyn or Long Island," I explained to Bob.

"Oh, you thought that was the real Andy?" Bob said. "That's just a character he does: Andy Kaufman—nice, normal, sweet boy, and all that. That's not really Andy."

"Now I'm getting nervous," I said.

"Don't worry. You'll see. You don't *actually* have anything to be afraid of. Just be careful."

If that wasn't the real Andy, then that was the real Bob. But if that was the real Andy, then the warning from Bob was a trick and that Bob from a few minutes before wasn't the real Bob. Maybe Andy's parents were in on it, too. Maybe Andy's father was joking when he said Andy used to entertain at children's parties. These were scary thoughts.

At last Andy came out of the dressing room. He had on his blank stare.

"Your hair's not that blond," he said to me.

"It's mostly blond."

"Not blond enough."

"Enough for what?"

"Enough as I pictured it."

"Is it enough for me to write the story?"

"Oh, the story, right. Well, what do you want to do? These high school reporters are going to interview me for ten minutes. You can come to that. Then you can come over to my parents' house, where all their friends will be waiting at a party for me."

ANDY SAT down at a desk in a classroom and drank from two quart-sized bottles of juice. Some students stood around and asked him questions like "Who are your influences?" Even though Andy was always in a hurry and never had time for anything, he spent an hour with the students. "By the way, would anyone care for some juice?" he asked. He told them that when he was a child, his parents had taken him to a nightclub to see Elvis Presley and he believed that the singer was Elvis Presley. Around that time, he began to imitate the singer. It was only many years later that he realized the singer was an imitator of Elvis Presley and that he had been imitating the imitator all along.

"How did you feel when you realized you were imitating the wrong person?" one of the students asked seriously.

"Pretty bad. But I was just glad I could do anything. And nobody knew I was imitating the imitator, so it wasn't that bad."

Bob came into the classroom.

"Where have you been?" Andy said. "You're supposed to come and tell me our time is up so I have an excuse to get away. What kind of a road manager are you, anyway?" Then he stayed and continued talking to the students for another hour of questions. The questions and answers were more of the same, so I decided to wait outside in the hall.

WHEN THE time was up, I saw Bob carrying four big suitcases as he followed Andy out of the room.

"Take my juice, too," Andy said.

"How can I take the juice with all this?" Bob asked in a pathetic way.

"*You will take the juice. I need my juice,*" Andy said in a zombie voice.

"I can take the juice," I said.

"*No, Bob must take the juice,*" Andy said in the voice. "*He must carry everything. Leave him alone. He will manage.*"

Bob carried all the luggage through the parking lot to the car. "*Do not interfere,*" Andy said to me. "*It is not your place.*"

PARTY

IF YOU MADE me late for my mother's party, I'll be really angry," Andy told Bob in the car. "It'll be all your fault, all the blame on you."

"Me? Why me? You didn't have to sit there for an hour," Bob said.

"You were supposed to come for me! It was all arranged!"

"Come on! You mean you can't get away from high school kids? What is it, *Time* magazine? *The New York Times?* A bunch of teenagers, and he needs to be taken away from them!"

"When I need you, where are you? I ought to fire you on the spot!"

"This must be a joke," I said.

"Of course it's not. You were there. You saw what happened. You witnessed the whole thing," Andy said.

A crowd of mink coats was emerging from the house as we drove up. Some of the minks hugged and kissed Andy. One said, "You were so funny, I died laughing." Another said, "I have my eye on him for my daughter."

"Why is everyone leaving already?" Andy asked his mother.

"Andy darling, they've been waiting here for two hours," Mrs. Kaufman said. "Where were you?"

"Bob made me late," Andy said. "It's all his fault. See, Bob? You made me miss my mother's party. She went to a lot of trouble. She baked cakes and everything. All for me. It was in my honor and I wasn't even there."

"Come on, Andy, there are still lots of people inside," Andy's brother said.

"There are?" Andy said. "Well, let's try to make the best of it. But if Bob did his job, this wouldn't have happened."

It took Andy a long time to get into the house, because he stopped to talk to all the people who were leaving, one at a time.

Once inside a spick-and-span split-level house, Bob and I were shown into the dining room to a giant table filled with food—cakes, fruit, bread, cheese, and puddings.

"Is that all you want, grapes?" Mrs. Kaufman asked me.

"I'll have all the other things," Bob said.

I noticed that Andy had a small black plastic thing in his hand and pushed buttons on it every few minutes as he ran around from room to room.

"Are you taping me?" an intoxicated man asked Andy.

"Speak right into this, please," Andy said.

"You know that's illegal," the man said.

"Why does he want to tape these people?" I asked Bob.

"He tapes all kinds of things. That's what he does."

"And I didn't bring a tape recorder, because I thought it wouldn't be polite."

"He's probably taping you, too," Bob said.

"Andy, come eat," his mother called. "Bob, will you have some chicken soup? If you're vegetarians, this has vegetables—carrots, celery, and onions. And I put in *two* chickens.

"Don't tell anyone, but I put two cans of College Inn chicken broth into this, too," Mrs. Kaufman said to me. "They all think it's all homemade. Then I make clam chowder with this." She opened a cabinet to show me at least twelve or twenty cans of Doxee clam chowder.

"Then I add to it. Would you want to take some home with you? Andy, are you having soup?"

"I'm having everything. I'm a vegetarian, too. But in my mother's house I eat whatever I'm served," Andy told me as we sat down at the kitchen table. While he waited for his dinner, he sat in his chair in the style of a five-year-old child. He had tucked a large linen napkin into his shirt. His fist was on the table and a spoon was sticking up inside the fist. "Now what?" he asked.

Andy's mother brought him a plate of food. Everything on the plate was white—creamed chicken, white rice, and a pudding made from white noodles and sour cream.

"Can I please have some sour cream for the pudding?" he asked his mother.

"There's already sour cream in it."

"Could I have some extra to put on it?"

"I don't know why you need extra on it if it's made with it in it."

"Because I like some on it even though it's made with it in it."

"Do you ever eat green vegetables?" I asked Andy.

"When I'm home in L.A., I do. Here, look, I'm going to eat this salad," he said as small bowls of iceberg lettuce and slices of pink tomato were set out in front of us.

"What kind of dressing do you want?" Mrs. Kaufman asked. "We have all kinds." On the table were four bottles of different supermarket dressings—red, white, orange, and yellow. After Andy finished eating his completely white main course, he poured some white dressing onto his little bowl of salad and ate that. Then he went to the freezer and took out two pints of Häagen-Dazs ice cream and put them on the counter to unfreeze, as was recommended on the container at the time. After putting some ice cream into a bowl, he took it back to the table, where he sat down and began to stir. The stirring went on and on.

" WILL TONY Clifton be at Town Hall?" Bob asked Andy.

"I hope so. I hope we can get him."

"Who is Tony Clifton?" I asked.

"Oh, he's this Las Vegas nightclub singer, kind of a lowlife. But Andy gets Tony to open his act for him. I can't stand him myself."

"Whyyyy?" Andy asked, laughing. "I love him. I think he's great."

"He's kind of an underdog, so Andy likes to give him a chance," Bob said. "Most everyone hates him. What do you think of him, Mrs. Kawfman?"

"Who, Tony Clifton?" Andy's mother asked from her place at the kitchen sink. "I don't like him."

While he ate his ice cream, Andy asked everyone which hotel would be the quietest for him to stay at in New York. People were walking in and out of the kitchen.

"How about the Pierre?" someone said.

"Is it quiet?" Andy asked.

"Yes, you can get a quiet room."

"Will it be away from the elevator?"

"If you want."

"Will it have double doors?"

"If you want."

"Now I'd like some chocolate milk," Andy said. "Where's the syrup?"

"It's in the refrigerator," Mrs. Kaufman said.

Andy got up and opened the refrigerator. "I don't see it," he said.

"It's right on the shelf."

"Why does he want chocolate milk after ice cream?" I asked Bob.

"That's the way he is. Don't ask."

"Hey, smooda," Andy said to Bob. "Did you meditate yet?"

"Why does he call you smooda?" I asked Bob.

"That's my name."

"Spell it."

"*Z-m-u-d-a.*"

"Do you expect me to believe that?"

"What? It's true, it's my last name. Look, Kawfman, she thinks my name is a joke. I ought to be insulted."

"Let me see some identification," I said.

"What is this? Mrs. Kawfman, what's my last name?"

"Zmuda."

"You both got everyone to go along with it," I said.

"Are you cracking up already?" Bob said. "Usually it takes them a little longer. Kawfman, where do we usually have them sent?"

"Huh? Bob, you better go meditate before it's too late."

"I will, I will, don't worry."

"We're going to drive back to the city soon. You don't have much time left," Andy said as he stood up.

"Where are you going?" I asked Andy. I thought that this might be my last chance to talk to him.

"I'm going to the bathroom. You can come if you want. Wouldn't that be good for your story? Come on, walk me to the bathroom. I mean it. Just come here, don't be afraid. What did you want to ask me?" Andy was on his way down the hall. I was worried because he had his finger on his zipper.

"I'll ask you later."

"Come on, it'll be a great story."

"This isn't for the *Enquirer*," I said, and went back to the kitchen.

"What are they doing?" I heard Andy's mother ask.

"He's asking her to follow him to the bathroom," Bob said.

"That's going too far," she said.

"You should have gone," Bob said to me. "Pretend you're a reporter or something."

ANDY'S ROOM

I BETTER GO meditate before we leave," Bob said. "Maybe I'll just have some more cake first. These pants were once loose on me. But I'm not as bad as Kawfman. Did you see what he eats?"

"The only bad thing I do is sugar," Andy said.

After talking about sugar for a few minutes, we went to see Andy's room. It was a small room downstairs and it was filled with his possessions from his whole life. Magazines, books, puppets, boxes, and bags were strewn around and mixed up with clean clothes and laundry.

"Very nice," I said.

"I wanted this room," Andy said. "It's supposed to be the maid's room, but I made a deal with my parents to let me have it if I was going to live here the year after high school. They keep all my stuff for me here. Look, here's my Elvis collection—my pictures, magazines, articles. Here are my poems I wrote in high school." He pulled out some shopping bags filled with papers. "Here, all about Elvis. And here's the death bag. All about after he died. Want to see?"

"I have all that," I said.

"Do you have this—dead, in his coffin—in the *Enquirer*?"

"That one I didn't want."

"Why not? It'll be a collector's item someday! It already is."

"Don't you have any feelings?"

"Come on, what are you talking about? I have feelings, but I want to own a collector's item, too."

"Would you two stop arguing?" Bob said. "You just met, and you're always bickering. Let's maybe go back to the city."

"Well, I promised her she could see my Elvis things. And *you* didn't meditate yet. You're the real cause of the delay."

"I'll meditate in the car," Bob said.

HIGHWAY

I ASKED BOB if it was okay to let Andy drive. "Don't worry, I'll drive," Bob said. But as soon as we were finally settled in the car, I noticed that Andy was the driver and he was on the wrong side of the road. It was around 3 A.M. so there weren't many cars around, but there was snow and ice on the sides of the road, and always the chance of another car. Then Andy turned on the radio, took his hands off the wheel, and started to clap to the music.

"I don't think this is funny," I said.

"I keep telling you I'm not trying to be funny."

"It's not even interesting."

"He can't help himself," Bob said. "When he hears his music, he has to do it!"

"Let's turn off the radio then," I said.

"Okay, but I'll still hear it in my head," Andy said, and continued singing and dancing as he swerved the car around on the icy roads.

"Oh God, wait till he gets onto the highway!" Bob said. "Then he'll be speeding, too!"

"I know you two planned this, and it just isn't funny. I'm going to get out if you don't stop."

"You can't get out!" Andy said. "There's no place for you to go!"

"I'll call a taxi to come from New York."

"Look, what am I doing? I'm not doing anything. What's wrong with the way I'm driving?"

" 'Unknown comedians,' the obituary will say," I said.

"*Comedians?*" Bob said.

"If you kill yourselves before you're known, they won't get it right."

"I don't see anything wrong with the way I'm driving."

"Why can't Bob drive?"

"No, this is my parents' car and I can't allow anyone else to drive it."

"How could it be worse than the way you're driving?"

"You know you're insulting me?"

"Come on, Kawfman," Bob said. One of their fun things to do was to always pronounce Andy's last name wrong. "Cut it out. Let me just drive back to the city."

"Absolutely not! I'm getting angry now."

"We're almost at the highway," Bob said. "Once we're there, there'll be no stopping him! *Him* and his *music*! He can't help himself! It's a sickness with him!"

"You both don't know where to draw the line," I said.

"Do you think I'm one of those people who's *always on*? This is the way I drive," Andy said.

"Then I'm getting out. Stop here, and I'll get the police to take me to a phone." I undid the seat belt, and the car slowed down.

"Don't undo your seat belt! The car stops when you undo the belt!"

"Then take me to a phone."

"Okay, there's a gas station around here."

"Please stay on the right side of the road."

"Kawfman, would you grow up?" Bob said. "Let her call a cab."

"I'll let her if she closes the seat belt."

"I'll close it if you let Bob drive."

"I can't!" Andy yelled. "This is my parents' car and I promised them I'd take care of it! I gave them my word!"

"Andy, you are really insane," I said.

"Look, fasten the belt and I'll take you to the phone."

"Him and his music! God!" Bob said.

"You're both crazy," I said.

"We'll wait here for you while you call," Andy said calmly when we got to the phone booth. As I was dialing, Bob came and knocked on the door. "He promises he'll stop now. Come on back. He promised me he'd behave himself."

"I don't believe you. It's a trick."

"No, really, I convinced him that he went too far. He swore."

"No, I know you now," I said.

"Come on, I swear it. If he doesn't, you can just get out."

Back in the car, Andy drove a couple of blocks, then got onto the left side and started clapping his hands and tapping his feet.

"Okay, I'm getting out," I said.

"*What is wrong with my driving?* Just tell me! Put that seat belt back on!" The car slowed down again.

"Bob, I knew you were lying," I said.

"I can't control him."

"That's part of the act."

"Look, I'll drive you to a diner I know," Andy said. "You can call a cab from there. Then we can have some coffee while we're waiting for the cab to come."

"*Have some coffee?*"

"We're still friends, aren't we?" Andy said.

"I'll tell you when I see the diner."

"What about your story? What will you do?"

"Maybe you're a mad genius. I'll see you another time."

"There is no other time! This is it! I don't have any more time for you!"

"Then why did you screw it up like this?"

"*You* screwed it up! I was driving you all the way back to the city! We could have had fun! But you had to get afraid!"

"You're really crazy. We can't discuss this."

"Look, here we are. Didn't I say I'd take you to a nice diner?"

I was surprised to see that we were in front of a diner.

"Come on," Andy said. "I'll buy you coffee or tea, or anything you want. Zmuda, you haven't meditated yet!"

"Hey, you're right. There was too much commotion in the car. I know! I'll do it now, in the car, while you go in for coffee."

"Good idea," Andy said. "Let me talk to the cab company," he said as we walked to the diner. "If I tell them we're over the city line, it will be cheaper."

I stood with Andy at the phone and watched him make the arrangements for the cab to come. "Could you wait and give us a few minutes to relax and have some coffee?" he asked sincerely.

"It's better to tell them," I said. "If you ask them, they say no."

"They already said no," Andy said sadly.

He had a forlorn look as he stood at the phone waiting on hold. His white skin, his long black eyelashes, and his turquoise-blue eyes gave him the look of an otherworldly creature.

DINER

Two large orange juices," Andy said to the waitress. "Both for me. And the young lady will have tea."

"It's probably canned juice," I said.

"Is your juice canned or from a container or fresh?" he asked in that sincere style.

"It's concentrate," the waitress said.

"All right, then I'll have apple juice. I make fresh juice when I'm in California, on my own juicer," he said to me.

"You could eat more vegetables and fruit. Don't you learn that with the meditation thing?"

"My maharishi says sugar is okay."

"How can that be?"

"What's so bad about sugar? Do you think I need to lose weight?"

"Your face would get thinner."

"How do you lose weight from your face? I never heard of that. I need my ice cream."

"Here comes Bob," I said.

"Shhh. Don't say anything," Andy said.

Bob ignored us at our booth and sat down at the counter. A big, white-haired man came over to him and said, "You're in my seat!"

"Who says!" Bob yelled.

"I says! That's my seat you're in!"

Bob and the man began to argue as the other customers and the diner employees looked on. All of a sudden Bob started to cry. "So I accidentally took a guy's seat!" he said in between sobs. "How was I supposed to know?" The counterman and the other diner patrons came over and tried to comfort him. I was alarmed to hear Andy call out in the zombie voice, "Imagine that, a grown man crying! I'm disgusted."

"Who asked you?" called the white-haired customer, who was now standing over Bob in a sympathetic way. Andy looked ahead with a blank stare and said, even louder, "A grown man crying! I'm ashamed for the human race, I'm ashamed to be part of mankind!"

"You don't wanna be part of it, leave it!" the customer yelled .

"*You* leave it," Andy yelled back.

"Please stop, he's going to kill you," I said as quietly as I could.

"I'm afraid of no one! You think I'm afraid? Girls! Always afraid of something. A grown man crying is no better than a *girl*! *That's* what I say!" Then he said to me, "Wipe that smile off your face!"

"Could we get out of here?" I said.

"I'll get out of here all right. A grown man crying! I don't wanna be here for another minute."

"He thinks he's a big man just because he's got a girl with him," Bob sobbed as Andy and I got up to leave.

"Anyone's more of a man than a grown man who cries!" Andy yelled.

"Leave him alone, go on, leave already," called the customer. "He's okay here."

Bob got up, and on his way to the door he said, "Oh, I forgot my check."

"It's okay, forget it," said the counterman.

I watched Bob go out the door and do a wild dance to the parking lot. "Just 'cause he's got a girl with him!" he was shouting. "I'd like to see him without a girl. Then we'd see! You wait! How big a man will he be then?"

Andy and I got up and walked to the car while the restaurant people watched through the door. When we were all out of view, Bob got into the car with us, and he and Andy began congratulating each other.

"I bet you planned the whole thing," I said.

"How could we plan it? You saw the guy tell me I was in his seat," Bob said.

"You probably took his seat on purpose. You must have a plot for every occasion."

"Come on. It was brilliant improvisation," Andy said.

"What if the man had had a heart attack?" I said.

"Those are the risks you take," Bob explained.

"Don't you think it's cruel to manipulate innocent bystanders that way?" I said.

"What's cruel? You didn't like that?" Andy asked.

"I'd like it in a play or a movie."

"If you don't like that," Andy said, "I don't know what to tell you. Because doing that is my most favorite hobby in the world."

CABDRIVER

THE CABDRIVER WAS wearing an unrealistic black wig and said his name was Anthony Imbecilli. He was obviously part of the act. The plan was for him to follow Andy and Bob to Andy's house and wait for Bob to get his luggage so he could come back to the city to check into a hotel. I was alone with this driver in his car as we followed Andy and Bob in their car. The driver said he recognized Andy from TV, and since there were no psychiatrists handy, I decided to describe Andy's driving to him.

"You mean like this?" he said as he took his hands off the wheel and began to sing. I remembered *Diabolique* and how a person was actually frightened to death in that movie.

"Who's that, his wife?" said the driver after he finished his short, terrifying act.

"Where?" I said.

"The one driving," he said.

"I thought the one driving was Andy."

"Oh, I thought the blond guy was him."

"No, that's his co-writer or road manager or something."

"Oh. With the long hair, it looked like a woman driving," the driver said.

"Maybe they changed places," I said.

The driver radioed his supervisor to ask how much the extra detour back to Great Neck would cost. That proved he was a real cabdriver after all. "It would be good if you could get the name of our company into the story," he said. "My name, too—Imbecilli. Write it down if you want."

BACK IN Great Neck, while Bob got his luggage from the house, I tried asking Andy for more time.

"This was your time. You missed it," he said.

"You made me miss it. The whole thing is your fault."

"*The whole thing is* your *fault!* We could have had a really good time. Going in and out of different restaurants all night on the way to the city. You missed out. You refused to go. It was your opportunity to be with me. I don't give time to writers. This was a special favor."

"We just wasted about five hours."

"I know, and it's all your fault."

"Would you two stop bickering?" Bob said when he came out of the house. "Let's go. Kawfman, get some sleep. I'll see you tomorrow."

"Okay. And meditate tomorrow before it gets too late," Andy said. Then he gave me a hug and a kiss good-bye. I figured it was some show business thing that was done no matter what the circumstances.

"We're still friends, aren't we?" he said.

"You know I love you, but you're really insane," I said.

Back in the cab, Bob warned me, "He tapes everything. He taped you saying you loved him. He'll get you to bring your husband to meet him at Town Hall and he'll play the tape onstage. He'll splice it out of context. That's what he does—he's a maniac. I was trying to warn you when you were kissing good-bye in front of the garage, but now it's too late. He has everything on tape."

"What for?"

"To torture people. To get a reaction. He has a sadistic streak. He can't have a real girlfriend, because he'll tape the most intimate moments and play the tape at a party. No girl will have anything to do with him. You'll see. Wait till your husband hears those 'I love you' tapes and the sounds of the hugs and the kisses."

"He loves Andy, too. He'll know what it was."

"Can you count on that? He better be a pretty understanding guy."

All I wanted was to see whether the cabdriver was taking us to New York. I was surprised when we got to my house. He said he'd like a ten-dollar tip, even though the fare was twenty-five—all for him since it was his own cab. "And mention the cab company," he said a few more times. I didn't get it. We pay the fare and we have to mention the company. It was five-thirty and the sun was beginning to come up. I hoped the super wouldn't see me coming in.

TOWN HALL

BEFORE TONY CLIFTON came out onto the stage to open the show, an announcer asked the audience to refrain from smoking. Since smoking wasn't permitted at Town Hall anyhow, this seemed an odd request.

Tony Clifton was wearing the same kind of toupee as Anthony Imbecilli had worn. He had a big paunch that seemed to weigh him down and make him walk in a lopsided way. The toupee, the thin mustache, the paunch, and the shiny tuxedo—these things made me wonder who Tony Clifton was. "It's Andy," people sitting around me said. Then Tony lit a cigarette and said, "That's right, *I* can smoke, *you* can't. It's *my* act, I do what I want!" The voice wasn't Andy Kaufman's voice but a new low-life voice that went with the Tony Clifton look. The song he sang was "My Way," with the lyrics "I've tasted life, I chewed it up . . ." He somehow made these lyrics sound even worse than they ever had before. The audience of kids, aged eighteen to thirty-five, was applauding, laughing, and screaming.

Tony Clifton called for volunteers from the audience to come up onto the stage. I noticed that Bob was among them. Tony was rude and mean to all the volunteers, but he was the meanest to Bob. He got Bob to tell that his name, Zmuda, was Polish. Then Tony told a Polish joke, and after the joke he poured a glass of water over Bob's head. Bob quickly got to the crying stage. Then he ran down off the stage and then ran all the way up the aisle and out of the auditorium.

I remembered hearing Andy say, "Tony Clifton is a terrible male chauvinist." "I say a woman's place is in the home," Tony Clifton told the audience at Town Hall. "If she wants to work, let her work in the kitchen! Women can peel the potatoes, they can wash the dishes if they want to work." Women in the audience began to yell back at him. He challenged one of them to come up onstage, and when she did they got into a fistfight, which she won.

After a while Tony was booed off the stage. People were screaming for Andy Kaufman. "Awright, you want Kawfman, you'll get Kawfman," Tony said.

The intermission went on for half an hour. In the auditorium, tapes were played of phone conversations between Andy and his mother and Andy and his grandmother. "You never call me," Andy's mother said on tape. "Andy, Andy, what do you want from me?" his grandmother said after Andy asked her a number of questions over and over.

Somehow, during the intermission I was introduced to Andy's manager. I could see that he didn't consider my project to be of any importance. Then his date asked whether the story was for *Harper's Bazaar.* When I said no, *Harper's Magazine,* she quickly lost interest.

For the opening of the show, Andy danced onto the stage as he sang "Oklahoma." Then he did the same act he'd done at his high school and a real audience with grown-ups liked the show as much as the high school audience. When I asked Andy later how he'd chosen his last song, with the lyrics "In this friendly, friendly world with each day so full of joy, why should any heart be lonely?" Andy said he just liked the song. "It's an old Fabian hit," he said.

After the show was over, I found Andy collapsed in a chair in his dressing room. His face was red and he had a blank look. I went back downstairs to the stage. I saw the blond-haired girl who'd knocked out Tony Clifton. She was sitting on a table. The stage was being set up with large tables of food ordered from a Chinese restaurant.

"All his parents' friends and relatives from Great Neck are here," Bob explained. "It's another party."

"Oh, I thought that was a joke when you told me that a party would take place here."

"I never joke around with you," Bob said.

I saw Andy's mother supervising the preparations for the party. I went over to that part of the stage and asked if she'd have time sometime to talk about Andy. "Of course," she said. "We'll meet for lunch in the city."

"Oh good," I said, even though I was thinking it would be better to meet for tea. The word *lunch* scared me almost as much as the word *pants* had when Andy had said it to me. The thought of going to midtown Manhattan when so many others are out and about, jamming into restaurants—the thought of this scene filled me with dread. "I don't know whether Andy will talk to me again," I said. "He says I missed my chance because I didn't like the way he was driving us back to New York last week."

Andy's mother stared at me and smiled. It didn't look like a normal smile. I wanted to describe the incident without seeming to say anything bad about her son, but it wasn't possible.

"Don't you realize that with Andy it has to be fun?" she said. "He won't do it if it's not *fun*."

I looked at her and I couldn't believe that if she knew the facts she would condone driving on the wrong side of icy roads.

Then I went back upstairs. In the dressing room, Andy had recovered and was packing up his puppets and drums and putting everything he could fit into a battered suitcase. He was folding each thing neatly. "I have no time for you now!" he yelled at me. "What do you want?"

"Just an hour anytime during the week."

"An hour! I don't have an hour. Do you know how busy I am? Do you know all the things I have to do this week? I have to see people, make phone calls—what magazine is this for again?"

"An hour goes by so quickly."

"I might get to see the reporter from *Rolling Stone*," he yelled as he rushed around packing.

"Do you work for *Rolling Stone*?" the blond girl asked from her new spot leaning against the wall of the dressing room.

"That would be good," Andy said. "What I do isn't for intellectuals, I'm in show business! I'll try to call you during the week. But I'm not promising anything. *If* I have time. *If.* You had your chance with me the other night. You

had the whole night. You had hours. You missed your opportunity. It's all your fault! You could have had the whole
story! We could have had *fun*. But you wouldn't stay in the
car with me! You had to take a taxi! You had to insult my
driving! You wouldn't drive with me!"

"That was your fault," I said.

"It was your fault," Andy said.

"What are you two arguing about?" asked Bob as he
came into the room.

"She ruined her chance to talk to me by leaving us the
other night and now she's bothering me for more time. Go
downstairs and join the party, both of you!"

HOTEL ROOM

ANDY WAS STAYING on in New York for a few weeks to appear on *Saturday Night Live,* and whenever I called him at the hotel, his phone was busy. Later he told me that half the day he was sleeping. Then he was on the phone. Then he was meditating and the phone was off the hook. Then at four o'clock when there was no answer, he was out. "I have to rush out and do all my errands and get everywhere in the one hour left before they close," he explained.

I waited a few hours at the NBC studios for my appointment to talk to Lorne Michaels about Andy. I had the simple idea that people who worked with Andy knew what he was doing, and if I asked them, they would tell me and I would understand. While I waited for the producer, I decided to try Andy's line at the hotel again. When

I told Andy where I was, he said, "I'm very flattered that you're going to all this trouble to find out about me. You actually went to talk to Lorne Michaels just about me? That's very nice."

"But I have no other reason to talk to him. I'm dreading it, as a matter of fact. Let's make a time to meet so I can get off his phone," I said. This was in the era when people had to use other people's phones. Phones on desks.

"You talked to him about me already?"

"Yes, a little. But he left to see the rehearsal and he's on his way back here any minute, so I have to go."

"What did he say about me?"

"Only good things. I'll tell you later."

"Like what?"

"There are other people here now."

"Like who?"

"Like the secretary, a producer, and others."

"Okay, let's go out to dinner for the interview time. First I have to watch the end of this program and then I have to meditate. Call me in an hour. If the line is busy, I'm still meditating. Where should we go? What restaurants are open late at night, do you know?"

"I'll find out."

"Who's there now?"

"Same ones, and footsteps are getting closer."

"Where are you, right in the office?"

"Yes."

"At his desk?"

"Sort of. I'll see you later. Okay?"

"Okay, but I'm trying to picture where you are."

"Can I tell you later?"

"Okay, but call in an hour and a half because this show is over and I want to watch the next one."

BY THE time Andy answered the phone about seven hours later, it was 11 P.M. "When I get involved watching television, I can't turn it off," he explained. "Then I had to meditate. You come up here, because I can be finishing some things while you're on your way."

"But aren't we going downtown?" I said. "That's where they'll be open late."

"I want to go to a real restaurant. Will they be real restaurants?"

"What do you mean, 'real'?"

"You know, the kind of place with real waiters. Waiters with foreign accents, waiters who carry a napkin over their arms. A fine restaurant. I want to go to the kind of place my parents would take me to."

"Is this a joke?"

"No, why?"

"There are real restaurants downtown."

"Do they have lobster tails?"

"They have lobster."

"But do they have lobster tails?"

"I don't know. Isn't it better to have a whole lobster?"

"I want lobster tails. They're better."

"There is a restaurant that has vegetables and brown rice, and I think they have fish and lobster."

"But do the waiters have accents?"

"No, mostly it's kid waiters. Actors and things."

"No, that's not what I want," Andy said.

"They must have lobster."

"Lobster tails?"

"They're all going to be closed if we keep talking about it."

"I know a place that's open late! My parents took me there. It's the right kind of place. Joe's Pier 52. They have lobster tails and everything."

When I called Andy from the lobby of the Essex House, he answered in an English accent and said he wasn't there. When I called back a few minutes later, he said, "Come up and wait for me while I finish my application to a meditation retreat. You can watch television."

"But there's nothing to watch on television," I said.

TWILIGHT ZONE

Hurry up, come in," Andy said at the door. "I'm watching *The Twilight Zone.*"

"I can't stand that," I said.

"What! How could you not stand it? It's the best show ever on, practically. You don't like Rod Serling?"

"I applied to the college he went to and he was always mentioned as a famous alumnus."

"So what's wrong with that?"

"It made me think about going to a different college."

"Look, this woman is really hundreds of years old. It's the same actress, see, none of her family knows how old she is, but soon we'll get to see her age. I've seen this one a few times."

"Don't you think you should try to get ready? It's almost midnight."

"The restaurant stays open till one, I found out. Okay, I'll do this thing while I listen to the show."

Andy sat down at a table covered with papers and twenty or thirty bottles of vitamin pills.

"By the way, why do you meditate?" I asked.

"It keeps me calm," he said while tapping his foot up and down and rapping his fingers on the table.

"I'm makin' like I'm nervous," he said without looking up from his papers. "Get it? It's a joke. Let's see: New York address, Los Angeles address, how many years have I lived here, three, how many years have I lived there, now I put this in here and this in there. Do I have everything?"

"Why didn't you do this before?"

"I was busy watching television. I got engrossed. Don't bother me, go sit down and watch this fantastic show."

"I can't believe you really like *The Twilight Zone*," I said.

"Of course I do! I suppose you're one of those people who think *Mary Tyler Moore* is the greatest show on TV. Okay now, just shut up while I do this. You know, you should be very flattered, I treat you like a member of my family, like a wife or mother or sister. I can yell at you and do whatever I want."

"It doesn't feel flattering."

"Well, that's because you don't appreciate it. Mostly with people I'm shy and quiet. Okay, I'm finished. Now let me tell you how much I love *The Twilight Zone.*"

"Because you think it's surrealistic?"

"How did you know?"

"You already told me."

"Okay, and what's my favorite movie?"

"American Graffiti."

"Right! And what's my favorite other movie that's a foreign movie?"

"8 ½."

"And how many times have I seen it?"

"Eight and a half times?"

"No, sixteen times. And in what movie do I identify myself with the hero?"

"The Graduate."

"Wasn't it just like *The Graduate* the other night at my parents' house?"

"No."

"Why? How could you say no?"

"Because you're not a graduate with a promising future."

"But they think I might be a Hollywood star," Andy said in a sad way.

"But Hollywood is a place where a lot of nuts go."

"Yeah, but didn't you see the resemblance of that party to the party in *The Graduate*?"

"Yes, but I saw no resemblance between you and the graduate."

"You're too literal-minded. Okay, I'm going to call the restaurant to make sure they know we're coming."

"Can you go in those clothes?" I looked at his white bell-bottom pants and gray sweatshirt.

"I'll ask," he said. He called and asked in his English accent, "Can we wear blue jeans?" even though neither of us was wearing blue jeans.

"We can dress informally," he said when he'd hung up. "Okay, come here. I want to show you something."

"What is it?"

"Come through here into the bedroom to the bathroom. Just trust me. It'll be worth it."

"I would never trust you."

"Come on, into the bathroom. I'm going to turn out the light for a second and close the door."

"I'm not going in there with the light out and the door closed. You'll probably lock the door and check out of the hotel."

"Don't be stupid. Just do what I say."

"There isn't even any window in the bathroom to call for help."

"Why are you so suspicious of me? Come on! Your last chance! Get in there or you'll be sorry."

"Absolutely not," I said.

"Okay! You won't go into the bathroom. Then you can leave! No bathroom, no trusting me to show you something worthwhile, then no hour alone with me! No dinner tonight. No story for you. Come on. Out! Get out! I mean it! Get out of my room and go home!"

"Okay, let me get my things."

"No, no things, out without things! Go on, get out!"

"I'm not leaving without my coat."

"Coat! Come on! Out, out, out, before I get angry!"

I gathered up my coat and notebook and tape recorder. "Good-bye," I said.

"Good riddance!" Andy yelled, and slammed the door behind me.

As I waited for the elevator and wondered how I might describe this episode to anyone, Andy's door opened. He was smiling. "You believed that?" he asked. "Come on, come back in. Are you crying? Come here, let me comfort you."

"I'm certainly not crying. I'm tired. I don't usually stay up all night."

"Okay, I'm not really mad at you. But the truth is you missed out on something great."

"What was it?"

"You should have come if you wanted to see. But you didn't trust me, so you missed it. It was really funny, too, and you're always liking things to be funny."

"I wish I knew what it was."

"Well, now you'll never know. Shall I get my coat so we can go to dinner?"

"Wasn't that the plan?"

"I thought you might change your mind and we could stay here and have a love affair. I mean, if you weren't married we could have."

"If I weren't married I still would never get involved with you."

"Why, what's wrong with me? You're always telling me how nice and talented I am."

"I never said nice."

"Well, you like me though."

"I like you as a brother or a cousin or a discovery from another planet."

"Oh. Well, I wouldn't touch a married person anyway. I once did kiss a girl who was married. Her husband was right there and said they had some new kind of marriage, like open marriage or something, and he said it would be all right, he wanted me to kiss her, he said to do so and so I did so, and she was a real good kisser, too, it was one of the best kisses I ever had, and then you know what happened? The next day I tore a ligament in my foot. It was like a punishment. So I'll never kiss a married woman. I know now that it's a sin."

"Good. Let's go."

"Oops. I better call, because it's twelve forty-five now. I'll tell them we'll be right there and see if they'll take us."

"I don't think it's good to get there at five to one if they close at one."

DINNER AT 1 A.M.

Don't you say 'Thank you'?" Andy said to the cabdriver. "The next time a cabdriver doesn't say 'Thank you,' I'm going to take the tip away from him," he said to me.

"You might lose your life."

"Wouldn't it be worth it, though? What time is it?"

"Five to one."

"We have a reservation—I called earlier," Andy said to the maître d' in the English accent.

"The kitchen just closed."

"I'm very sorry, but I just phoned and was told I would be served if I arrived before one."

"It is almost one now," said the maître d'.

"Almost—but not yet one. I made a reservation, I made

a special trip over here, and now I require that you serve us," Andy said.

After a few more minutes of this discussion, a person in charge was called and Andy had the same conversation with him. Finally, they agreed and the maître d' took us to a table.

A waiter came over and said, "Our kitchen is closed. All I can get you is coffee and dessert."

"Go speak to your employer. He promised us a dinner," Andy said.

"Aren't you afraid they might poison the food or something?" I said.

"What do you mean? You don't believe I'm really angry?"

"If you're angry, why are you talking in an English accent?"

"I can be angry in any accent. I have to stay in character, but I was very angry. I demand to be treated respectfully. You should always believe me when I'm in an angry fight with someone who doesn't treat me with the proper respect."

The waiter came back and said, "What will you have?" Then Andy asked him some questions about the menu. He asked every question that could be asked. "What kind of fish is this? . . . I see, and what is this soup? . . . What is this shrimp? . . . Do you have lobster tails? . . . How are they prepared? . . . Is that with red sauce?" Then he ordered his dinner. "I'll have the soup, the salad, and the lobster tails, and may I have rice instead of a potato?"

"Very good, sir, I'll see what I can do."

"Have whatever you like. I want to pay for dinner," Andy said.

"I'm paying for the dinner," I said. "It's part of the job."

"I want to do something nice for you," Andy said.

"You are—the interview."

"Wouldn't it be funny if we fell in love?"

"Very funny."

"You know why, because, little by little, I'm falling in love with you."

"Not that funny."

"Okay, I'm not really falling in love with you, but wouldn't it be fun? What would we do? Would we go to the top of the Empire State Building and ride the Staten Island ferry and walk in the streets eating ice cream like couples in love are supposed to do?"

"Is that what people do?"

"Wouldn't it be fun to do those things as a couple in love?"

"No."

"Why, have you done them already?"

"I've never done any of them and I don't want to."

"Why not? I do. I want to do everything I missed when I was too shy." Then he closed his eyes and silently said grace, or pretended to—I couldn't be sure.

"I think I just saw Muhammad Ali," Andy said when he finished grace. "He comes here a lot. Big celebrities come here. You know that his birthday is the same day as mine? And Elvis Presley is one week before mine?"

"You told me that the first time we talked on the phone."

"I did? What did you say?"

"I think I said, 'So what?' "

"No, you were very impressed by the fact, probably."

"I don't live in California, so I don't care when people's birthdays are, unless they're on the same exact day. Maybe then I'd care for a second."

"I'm from New York, too, you know," Andy said. When I looked up from my salad, which I was afraid to taste, I saw that Andy had a big drop of tomato sauce on his chin. I guessed that he had gotten it there on purpose. "You have a drop of sauce on your chin," I said.

"Oh," he said, and took his red linen napkin and wiped it off. He found the place right away. "Thank you for telling me," he said seriously.

During this dinner, I kept trying to find out from Andy how he got to be the way he was. "Don't ask me questions like that," he said. "I just did. I did things in my room and then I did them at children's parties and then I did them in college and then I did them at the Improvisation and then I got discovered for *Saturday Night Live* and then I went to L.A. All right? Is that what you want to know? Can you write your story now? Look, no more stupid questions. I'm having my dinner. Oh that's right, you're paying for it. Okay. Well, after we finish dinner we'll walk over to the Improv and see if Bob is there. Then you'll see where I got my start, okay? By the way, what did Lorne Michaels say about me?"

"Nothing much," I said.

"You talked to him for twenty minutes and he didn't say anything about me?" Andy said.

"Hardly anything."

"What did he talk about, then?" Andy said.

"About himself," I said. "And about what kind of thing he thinks is funny."

"He talked about himself?" Andy said. Then he laughed.

"He said he didn't like waiting for half an hour during the intermission at Town Hall. He said his time was valuable. But I had to wait for him at NBC for three hours."

"What did you do while you waited for him?" Andy asked.

"I watched part of the dress rehearsal and asked people about you."

"You did? Who did you ask about me?"

"I watched Dan Aykroyd do that 'bad theater' thing he does, then asked him what he thought about what you do."

"Do you like that 'bad theater' thing?"

"I like what he does. Don't you?"

"I don't do what they do so I'm not in a position to say. I'm not trying to be funny. What did he say about what I do?"

"Mostly he talked about himself and what he does."

"These people are busy with their own careers. You have to realize that."

"Don't they have a minute to wonder about what you do?"

"They have their own work. That's show business. You have to accept it. Who else did you ask about me?"

"The others who were rehearsing."

"And what did any of them say?"

"They said, 'Yeah, Andy's great,' and then they talked about their own work."

"It's your job to wonder about things because you're a writer. They're in show business."

"They could wonder about you for a second."

"Lorne Michaels said he didn't like waiting at Town Hall? How could he say that? Didn't he like the tapes I played of my grandmother talking?"

"He didn't say. He just kept saying his time was valuable."

"Well, he's a busy man," Andy said. "Very, very busy."

On the walk over to the Improv, Andy told me a few new things. "I'm not a comedian. What I am is a song-and-dance man. And if someone wants to really flatter me and be complimentary, they could call me an absurdist and a surrealist. Because I'm not trying to be funny. I hate when they analyze what I do."

CHERRIES

A FEW DAYS later Andy made an arrangement for me to meet him and Bob at NBC before Andy's appearance on *Saturday Night Live*. When I arrived, Bob was sitting at a desk in the hallway. He was shouting into a phone: "Well, I'm sorry Mr. Kawfman is in the hospital with a heart attack. Andy has to go on live TV; he can't be running to the hospital. . . . Where's your *other* son, Mrs. Kawfman?" People going by were looking at Bob in disbelief.

After he'd hung up, Bob and I waited around outside Andy's dressing room for a while.

"That Kawfman, always late. Let's go to the lobby and get some coffee or something."

We found a coffee shop in the lobby.

"Look at those maraschino cherries," he said as we sat down at the counter. "Aren't they disgusting? You could probably get cancer just from looking at them."

"Just think how many we ate during our childhoods," I said.

"I don't want to. Let's see, now. What should I have, I guess I'll just have something to drink after all."

"What will you folks have?" the waiter asked.

"Well," Bob said, "you know what I would really like? You see those cherries over there?"

"Those for the sundaes and things?" the waiter said.

"Well, yes, whatever you use them for. I just love them. They are my favorite thing in the whole world. Do you think I could get just a few of those?"

"Well, I'd like to help you, sir, but those aren't sold for eating, they're just to put on top of things decoratively, like on sundaes, you know, or on a grapefruit half or on an ice cream soda."

"Oh, please," Bob said, looking with desperation at the cherries in a giant jar. "I don't care what it costs, I'll pay the price, five dollars, ten, a hundred."

"Well, I don't know," said the waiter.

"Just a few in a bowl . . ." Bob said, staring at the cherries.

"I could give you one or two," the waiter said.

"No, no, I need to have a bowl full. Just five or six or ten in a little bowl. I'd be grateful to you if you'd just arrange to put some in a little bowl."

"Well okay, I guess, if I don't tell anyone."

"Oh God, thank you so much," Bob said, still staring at the cherries and beginning to chew on his napkin in a wild way.

"And what would you like to drink?" the waiter asked him.

"Nothing, nothing, just the cherries, oh! Okay, anything, a Coke, a Tab, anything."

"A bowl of cherries and a soda," I said. "Very nice."

The little bowl came filled with cherries. "Oh God, thank you so much," Bob said. "May I please have the sugar?" Then he took five or six packages of sugar and poured them over the cherries.

A woman was sitting next to Bob at the counter. She looked over at the cherries. She had the appearance of a tourist who was visiting Rockefeller Center. She was about thirty-five or forty. She was pale and thin and she had brown hair with a ribbon around her head. She wore harlequin eyeglass frames and she wore a loden coat from around 1959. She had the look a number of people had at the time, the look of having just been released from a state mental institution.

"Here," Bob said, holding out a spoonful of cherries to the woman. "These are really delicious," he said to her. "They are! Here, have a taste."

"No, thank you," she said.

"Really, they're so good. Come on, just try it—how can you know if you don't try it?"

"No, I don't want any."

"Please, just one."

"No, I really don't want any," she said in a panicked voice.

"That's enough," I said to Bob.

"Why? They're so good. I love them more than anything."

"I'm going to leave in a second," I said.

"How much tip should I leave the guy?" Bob asked.

"At least five. You didn't even eat any."

"How could I eat them? Look," he said, taking a spoonful of wet pink sugar from the cherry bowl. "Doesn't it look disgusting?"

ANDY ARRIVED at seven-fifteen. He was in his good mood that came from just having meditated.

"Hi," he said. "Did you and Bob have fun together?"

"Do you know what he did?" I asked.

"What? Something great?" Andy said.

"Do you know about the cherries?"

"No, but I do know Bob is great. Didn't I tell you what a good actor he is? Isn't he the funniest man in the world?"

"Yes, but what about you?"

"I'm not trying to be funny. Hey, Zmuda, she talked to Lorne for twenty minutes to find out about me and he talked about himself."

"C'mon, what did he say?" Bob asked me.

"He talked about his ideas about which kinds of things are funny," I said.

"He talked about his own ideas? Great!" Bob said. He and Andy started laughing. "He's a producer," Bob said. "What do you expect?"

"Hey, where is that picture of you when you had blonder hair?" Andy said. I handed him my passport. "Let's see, oh great, I see it's true. It used to be all blond, you were telling the truth. You know what, when I first saw you I thought you were some dowdy writer, but you could really look good if you wanted. You should dye your hair all blond and wear tight pants like they do in California."

"But I'm not trying to be a movie star."

"That's not the style here, Kawfman," Bob said.

"Why, look how good it would look," Andy said, taking some corduroy from the sides of my slacks and pulling it back the way tailors do, so we could all see in the dressing-room mirror. "There, that's how they should be. You know what you remind me of—there's a girl in this Elvis Presley movie wearing glasses and baggy clothes and her hair is pulled back, and she's a drummer, a girl drummer, and then she takes off the glasses and changes into some tight clothes and curls her hair. You know how in all the old movies there's always some dowdy girl who gets transformed? That's what you remind me of."

"She doesn't wear glasses," Bob said.

"But she tries to make herself look plain and dowdy on purpose."

"That's the style here," said Bob. "We don't have that in California."

"Everyone there wants to be a movie star," I said.

"In New York they want to be serious," Andy said. "That's their problem. It's not as much fun."

ANDY'S PLAN for the show that night was to read from *The Great Gatsby*. He showed his costume to Bob and me. It was a black tuxedo and a dark-yellow polyester shirt with ruffles down the front. "This is my father's shirt," he explained. "I chose it because it's the kind of shirt I think Gatsby would wear."

"Maybe you should read over the description of his shirts," I said.

"Why—what's wrong with this shirt?"

For the dress rehearsal, Andy came out onto the stage and addressed the audience in the English accent. He said he'd been given permission to do anything he wanted for the last twenty minutes of the show and he had decided to come out as his real self and read from *The Great Gatsby*.

After a couple of minutes of the reading, the crew and the audience began to boo. Andy asked whether they'd all like to hear him read more or play some music on a record player he had behind him. All chose the music, and he put the record on. It was Andy's voice reading what he'd just read.

After the rehearsal, Andy said he was worried about how the act would go over. "Am I blowing my whole career on this?" he asked Bob in the hallway. "Should I just go out there and play my drums?"

John Belushi walked by and complimented Andy on the reading. Then he stopped and said, "I saw Tony Clifton. That was really great."

"Oh, I don't do Tony Clifton anymore," Andy said. "Where'd you see him?"

"I just saw you do him recently," John said.

"That was really him," Andy said. "I used to do Tony Clifton, but now I get the real Tony Clifton to come and be himself."

"What? You mean for religious reasons or something?"

"No, he got mad, he didn't like me doing him, so I had to stop, and now I get him to appear at my shows whenever he can."

"Oh," John said. Then he gave Andy the look Humphrey Bogart had when he was told that the casino was being closed because gambling wasn't allowed.

BACK IN the dressing room, Andy said to me, "Please scream. You know, like you're being attacked."

"That wouldn't be right," I said.

"Come on, scream—I'm just trying to do something."

"You'll scream," Bob explained, "and then he'll dash out into the hall and act normal."

"I don't want to be part of it," I said.

"Come on, hurry, scream. Okay! I'll scream myself. Eeek! Eeek! Okay, here I go."

"What is he doing?" I asked.

"I don't know. Here—have a piece of fruit," Bob said as he passed me the NBC complimentary fruit basket.

"Hey, I know," Andy said on his way out the door. "I could put a banana peel on the floor and pretend to slip on it. That would be funny, wouldn't it?"

Half an hour before he was scheduled to appear on live television, Andy put on his white bell-bottom pants and a gray sweatshirt and told one of the producers he was going for a walk. "I'm just going to walk around the skating rink outside," he said. "I like to do it before I perform." The producer had a nervous look.

"I love to tell them I'm going out right before I go on," he told me. "I love to see their faces."

"What if something happened to you?" I asked.

"That's what I like—the element of danger. It's so exciting to go outside before a live show."

AFTER THE show, Andy was still worried. "What do you think? Did I blow the whole career?" he asked Bob a few times.

At the after-the-show party, in a restaurant, people complimented Andy on his performance. Some of them were well-known performers Andy liked to hear compliments from. "All the true artists appreciated it," Andy said when we sat down at a table. "But what about the rest?"

Then Charles Grodin came over to Andy and told him how much he liked Tony Clifton. Andy told him that he didn't do Tony Clifton anymore. When Andy went off to wash his hands, I asked Charles Grodin what he thought Andy was up to with Tony Clifton. "I don't know," he said. "I just don't know. Something about it doesn't seem right."

"I'M GOING to perform with the Sha Na Na's in Philadelphia for a few days," Andy told me a few days later. "You can come to Philadelphia and if I have time I'll talk to you. But you have to promise not to get in the way."

"How would I get in the way?"

"Well, we might be trying to get girls and then you'd cramp our style. But that won't be a good place for girls anyway, so I think it's safe for you to come."

When I called Andy at his hotel in Philadelphia, he had forgotten all about the plan. "Oh, that's right! You were supposed to come here. Well I was wrong, there are plenty of girls here. A plentiful supply, so you would definitely be in the way. But I'll be back in New York in June and then maybe I'll have time for you. The point is I'm planning to be busy all the time here. Last night we had two girls in our room and they weren't too pretty, okay, and then they said they had to leave. 'We have to study,' they said. The next night they sent their boyfriends to come beat us up. Two big football captains. But we outsmarted them."

ALBANY

In JUNE, ANDY was away at his meditation retreat. When he got back home to California, he told me that he couldn't come to New York because of some great news. "I have a part in a new series done by the people who did *Mary Tyler Moore* and all those shows. It's going to be a big hit! I'm a mechanic who can't speak any English."

"I thought you hated those shows," I said.

"But my manager says it'll be good for my career. I'll get well known and my special can get aired! I have to do it."

He had a new idea for a time we could meet in New York. "I come every August to go to Coney Island and ride the roller coaster. My whole family goes. It's an annual family outing. Call my mother to see when I'll be arriving."

"I won't be in New York in the summer," I said. "This is the only thing I learned from psychotherapy."

"Well, if you want your time with me, that's when I'll be there."

WHEN I called Andy's mother to see if this was a true story, she told me that he really was coming to the city in August and the family was going to Coney Island. I didn't see how this could be the truth. "But New York is so hot and dirty in August," I said.

"He couldn't care less," she said, laughing. The idea that Andy would notice the weather seemed ludicrous to her.

"Your next chance for time won't come until October," Andy said when I spoke to him in September. "Then I'll be doing a tour of colleges and I'm going to Albany. You can meet me up there. But if you see I have a girl in my room and I'm about to score, please get out of the way. Don't try to ask me any of your questions."

IN OCTOBER, when I got to the Thruway House Motel in Albany, I made sure to get a room that wouldn't be too close to Andy's and Bob's. Then I went to the airport to meet their plane. Three bored students were waiting there to meet them and drive them around. I was surprised to see Andy coming down the long corridor wearing an ill-fitting dark-pink polyester suit jacket. His face was even whiter than usual. As he walked past us, he was squinting. "Is she here?" he said to Bob.

"You came!" he said to me after a few seconds. "Actually, this is nice seeing a familiar face. Usually we don't know anyone in these strange airports. But I'm in a terrible mood. Something really bad happened."

"What about the pink jacket?" I said. The pink polyester fabric was pilled, and bits of thread were sticking out all over.

"This is my jacket from *The Dick Van Dyke Show*. It was my costume."

"The shirt cuffs are attached to the jacket."

"It has sentimental value for me," Andy said. "What's wrong with it?"

"It has an unsavory look."

"I have worse problems than my jacket. Shall we tell her what happened, Zmuda? Can we trust her?"

"Well, you know how I feel. I think you should get over it already."

"I'm not getting over it. If you knew what they did to me. I can't think of the right word. It has to do with Tony Clifton. They hired him for a show—in the sitcom I have to do. I got him the part. How can I say it? What did they do? What's the word? You know, it's what one country does to another country in war. What's the word?"

"Invaded?" Bob said.

"No, no, somethinged something."

"Buffer zone?"

"No, no—come on. She'll know—she's the writer."

"What am I, chopped liver?" Bob said.

"Well, you're from California, you're in show business. She knows big words."

"Plummaged?" Bob said.

"No, no, that's not it. You know the word," Andy said to me.

"Kawfman, if we don't claim our luggage we'll lose it."

"Okay, but I have this character I've been working on for years," he said. He was talking in a whisper so the student greeters wouldn't hear. "And they did something terrible I can't forgive them for. Don't take my mood personally. I'm glad to see you. I appreciate your coming all the way up here."

"I got to see the leaves on the train ride. It's the foliage season," I said.

"It is?" Andy said. "Oh I want to see that. I never see anything in California."

"See—get your mind off it," Bob said. "Look at some leaves."

"I'll look at some after I decide what to do about this damage to Tony Clifton."

" SHE CAME all the way to Albany, Bob, we have to be nice to her this time," Andy said in the backseat of the students' van.

"Albany is the pits," one of the students said.

"I read that it's one of the worst cities in the world," I said.

"I don't mind," Andy said. "I'm here to perform."

When we got to the motel, we all realized that the rooms at the Thruway House were actually on the Thruway.

"My room isn't quiet enough," Andy said. "I know I'm going to be woken up. I need a cement wall between me and the next room. Let's see yours, Zmuda," he said. "Would you change rooms with me?"

"Sure, I want you to get sleep," Bob said.

"Where's her room? Maybe it's better."

"It took me an hour to check and make sure I had the quietest room," I said.

"Okay, would you change with me?" Andy asked.

"I would, but I'm afraid to be next door to Bob."

"Let's see, you have the cement wall, but you're close to the road," Andy said.

"All these cars outside will be starting their engines to check out at eight A.M., too," I said.

"Oh God!" Andy said. "All those terrible hours that people get up! I know they'll be waking me—I just know it! You must have the best room if you took an hour to check in."

AT A highway diner nearby, Andy found out that lobster wasn't available and he ordered shrimp instead.

"Diners upstate, away from the ocean, aren't the best places to order shellfish," I said.

"Why not? I always order shellfish wherever I go. Nothing's ever happened to me." Then he closed his eyes and said grace silently. I noticed that any meal set before Andy was given respect. Dinners in diners—frozen shrimp with canned tomato sauce, canned vegetables, salads made with the worst part of the lettuce. And then chocolate and vanilla ice cream for dessert. "I'll pay extra for it if I have to," Andy said to the waitress.

BACK IN his room after dinner, Andy fell into an armchair and said, "You came all the way here, so I'm going to talk to you now. I have a few things you'd love to know. But first, I see your hair is blonder. Or is it just from the summer? But you know what? It's not blond enough. It should be all blond. Every single hair should be bleached blond. Anyhow, here's what I have to tell you. There's this girl I'm in love with. I've been in love with her since high school—no, since seventh grade—and I was too shy to talk to her. Ever. She was one of the first beatniks, like you were, in high school, with the long hair and the black tights and all. And all these many years I've been yearning for her and thinking maybe someday I'll be famous enough to meet her. So here's what happened: Her father is in show business, I got to meet him and all, and I asked him about her, and it got arranged that we would meet. You know, I was so excited when the moment came, shivers ran up my spine, I was tingling with bliss . . ."

"And then you didn't like her?"

"No, I liked her, but it was no big deal. We didn't have that much in common. You know what? I meant to make up a story to tell you, but I accidentally told you the truth. If I'm so tired I'm telling you the truth, I better go to bed. Maybe we can talk tomorrow."

THE NEXT day at noon, when I walked outside past Andy's room, his curtains were wide open to the parking lot. He was lying in bed in a white terry-cloth robe and talking on the phone. I waved to him, and he opened the door. A chambermaid went by and laughed.

"I can't help it if everything I do looks funny," he said to me.

"He's just getting up," Bob said. "We have a two-hour wait." He had the door to his room open and was sitting in a chair in the doorway next to Andy's room. "I'm trying to get some fresh air," he explained.

"Why don't you go out for a walk?" I asked.

"Nah, I gotta wait for phone calls and get Kawfman to rehearsal on time. Look what a beautiful day it is. Isn't it great? You never see this in California. Is he dressed yet, or making any progress? Let's go look."

After a few visits from Bob, Andy got dressed. "How do I look?" he asked. "I know I'm sick, I have a cold or something, and I'm so tired. I need sleep."

"You need some fresh air and exercise," I said.

"How could I get any?"

"Go on a vacation."

"What would I do? I'd be bored in a few hours."

"Take one of your girlfriends with you."

"I wouldn't be interested in her for more than a few hours."

"Take someone you really like."

"What's the point of that? You mean some real relationship? Who wants to be with a sincere relationship on a vacation? You want to be with someone who looks good. I want to run around—at least I want to try to run around."

"You ought to go out and run around this parking lot a few times," I said. "Look how pale you are."

"You know what I mean. There's no one person I could be with unless it was Raquel Welch, then I'd know there was no way I could do any better than that. So I'd be satisfied. Maybe. I don't know."

"Do you ever do anything to stay healthy?"

"Yeah, sure. You know what I'm getting? One of those metal things with padding. It's a stand, and you stand on your head and the shoulders touch the pad and your head doesn't get hurt at all. It makes standing on your head easy."

"What's the point?"

"The point? According to literature, the point is . . . oh yes, plus I'm getting a slant board."

"I know what the point of that is."

"Well, it's the same point. To reverse gravity. Because all the years of your life, you've never reversed gravity, you're always the victim of gravity—I'm quoting from the literature now—and gravity, that's why people when they're older begin to sag, years and years of having gravity pulling down on you. If you can for a few minutes a day reverse the gravity . . ."

"Wouldn't you have to stand on your head an equal amount of time?" I asked.

"Noooo! You only have to reverse gravity a little bit. You lose your hair because of it, too."

"The blood doesn't run," Bob added.

"Yeah, so I got two things—I got the slant-board thing and the headstand thing."

"You still need to go on a vacation and get some sunlight and air," I said.

"I don't know how a vacation would agree with me. I don't do what people do on vacations. I can't go to a bar and drink."

"You could ride a bicycle. You could go hiking and swimming."

"I could go to the beach at Santa Monica if I ever had a few days off. I could go there, ride a bicycle, go swimming."

"He's in good condition," Bob said. "Look at his build."

Andy pulled up his T-shirt and showed us a soft white area.

"Very nice," I said.

"This is the way it really looks," he said as he tried pulling it in.

"I saw that! After you lifted your shirt, you sucked it in!" Bob said.

"Wait, it's good like this, though," Andy said.

"It's soft!" Bob said.

"It is not! Punch me. Just punch me! Feel that!" Andy said as he stood up. "It's hard. Look at Bob. He's fat!"

"I'm built like a bull!" Bob said.

"Let me see," Andy said. "Look, lookit that, he's suckin' it in now!"

"Take your shirt off," Bob said. "No, don't take it off, people get sick when he takes it off."

"I never saw anyone so white," I said.

"And the guy's got a tan now," said Bob.

"I know I'm pale and sickly!" Andy said. "This business is killing me!"

"What about last summer?" I asked. "For example, what did you do in New York last summer?"

"Did I go to New York last summer?" Andy said.

"LET'S GO!" Bob said. We were still in the room.

"Could I see the old pictures you got of me when I was

thin and handsome?" Andy said to me. I handed over some contact sheets I'd gotten from a photographer who was Andy's friend.

"Could we see the pictures *over breakfast*?" Bob asked. "Could we *get out*? No, don't show him. We'll never get out of here."

"Do I look like those old pictures now?" Andy said.

"You would if you lost a little weight," Bob said.

"Let me see," Andy said.

"Come on—come on, we gotta go, Kawfman."

"Why? I don't know how I got this way."

"Ice cream," I said.

"We're two hours behind schedule," Bob said.

The chambermaid came by and asked, "Can I clean up your room now?" She looked at Andy with admiration.

"Can we get to the restaurant through the motel?" Bob asked her.

"You don't come out no better neither way," she said.

"You can *go* around outside," I said. "Then you'll get some air."

WE WALKED through the parking lot from one part of the motel to the other. "Would it be all right if I left the tape on until you said to turn it off?" I said.

"Yeah, leave it on. Hey, Bob, she's going to leave it on until we say off. Have those syphilis sores cleared up yet?"

"Oh God," Bob said.

"Is the penicillin helping?" Andy said.

"Aren't you glad to be here at the peak of the foliage season?" I asked the two lunatics.

"Yeah, see the trees," said Bob.

"Yeah, I wish I could stay here a little longer. Not in Albany, but in the East. See, now here I could be with one girl where in California I couldn't. I could go driving up to New England. I did it once."

"Why can't you do it in California?" I said.

"Because California is different. It's a whole different consciousness."

"You mean you change your consciousness from coast to coast?"

"Wait a minute. I'm not talking about this. You know what you remind me of? 'Here's the door'—remember in that movie with Walter Brennan, *Meet John Doe*? 'They're gonna screw you up, get out of here!' "

"Yeah, let's go back on the road before she gets us good!" Bob said.

"You remind me of these two guys in a French movie, by Bertrand Blier. They act out their fantasies. Stealing and sex and all that."

"Like in *The Demon*?" Andy said. "That's my favorite book, by Hubert Selby, Jr. That's the story of my life."

IN THE restaurant, people were finishing lunch when we arrived for breakfast. "Can I sit on the end?" I asked when we got to a booth.

"You need to sit on the end, too—right, Andy?" Bob asked.

"Yeah. Then let's sit at a table with all ends."

"Why do you need to sit on the end?" I asked.

"Same reason you do," Andy said. Then he opened the envelope with the photographs of him. "These are the ones I'm really handsome in," he said.

"I don't think people want to see him handsome," Bob said. "He's supposed to be a schmuck."

"Wouldn't they like to see all the different ways he can be?"

"Can I look like this now?" Andy said.

"Sure you can," Bob said.

"Look at my broad shoulders in this one. So how can I look like that now?"

"What can we get them to give us at three o'clock in the afternoon?" Bob asked.

"Cereal? A banana?" Andy said. "You know what? Those students should have taken us to the diner for breakfast."

"We don't have time," Bob said. "We have an hour."

"That's not enough time to rehearse. Less than an hour with the drummer."

"Well, you were supposed to be there at two-thirty," Bob said. "It's your show. Your rehearsal."

"You know what?" Andy said. "I'm going to ask them if they'll make some eggs. I'll pay them to clean the griddle if they say they've cleaned it for the day. I'll pay them ten dollars extra to get eggs."

"Offer twenty," Bob said.

"I'd give them a hundred. But they won't do it. I've done this before, and they never say okay to making eggs."

"Go ask the hostess," Bob said. "She looks nice."

Andy went to negotiate.

"The hostess went to ask the cook," Andy said when he returned.

The hostess came to our table. "It's really terrible, but he said yes," she said.

"Okay, two plates of scrambled eggs, two large orange juices, two boxes of Raisin Bran, and two bananas."

"Do you have any grapefruit?" I asked.

"No, grapefruit juice."

"Frozen?"

"No, canned."

"Is the orange juice frozen, too?" I asked.

"It's concentrate, freshly made. It's real juice. It's not Tang."

"Do you think I could look like these pictures now? That Elvis Presley picture?" Andy asked when she'd gone.

"Sure," Bob said.

"How do you lose weight in your face? I thought you lose it in your stomach."

"You lose everywhere," Bob explained.

"Doesn't this look just like Elvis Presley?" Andy asked as he looked at a picture of himself.

"What about the fact that they don't know what orange juice is?" I said.

"What did she mean, 'concentrate'?" Andy asked.

"They take out the water and freeze the orange part," I said.

"Like somebody grabbing you and taking all the blood out of you and freezing you for the future," Bob said.

"Would you want to be frozen?" I said.

"Ridiculous," said Bob.

"Why?"

"Yeah, why?" asked Andy.

"Because when your body has enough, it's used up and that's it—your spirit goes to another body," Bob said.

"How can you be sure it does?" Andy said.

"I know for a fact it does. Energy is never destroyed, just altered."

"It really screws things up if you get frozen and returned to life, because what happens to your soul?" Andy said. "It doesn't work out."

"Maybe the soul freezes, too," I said.

"You know, I'm really sick," Andy said. "Ever since we've been on the road I'm sick. It's a feeling in my head. The only cure for it in my opinion is to get a lot of sleep, but I have no time."

"Go visit your grandmother in Miami next stop," Bob said.

"They have health-food stores there, too," I said.

"I stay with her," Andy said. "She makes canned peas."

"She could make you a salad." I said.

"Anything I want."

"Tell her you want a salad and vegetables," I said.

"I asked her. She says no. Oh, here come the eggs."

"I didn't have cream, so I brought half-and-half," the waitress said.

"At least it's not that fake cream," I said.

"I'd rather have *that*," Andy said.

"It's delicious," Bob said. "He turned me on to it in New Orleans."

"At home I have freshly squeezed juice from my own juicer, orange or carrot, then sprouts and tofu, then rice or barley and a baked potato, then steamed vegetables, then beans," Andy said. "And for breakfast I have freshly squeezed juice, orange or apple, then a pear or a peach, then sprouts that I grow myself, then tofu, then cottage cheese, then yogurt. Then after I finish with all that, I have cookies, candy, and ice cream."

"Do you notice anything about these eggs?" Bob asked.

"They're awful," Andy said, laughing. "Let's not eat them."

" 'They want eggs, we'll give them eggs all right!' the cook must have said—right, Andy?" Bob said.

"Look at me in this shot. Don't I look like some genial host of a talk show?"

"Maybe sometime you'll host the Johnny Carson show," said Bob.

"I think they think I'm just some crazy kid."

"How did they get that idea?" I said.

"I don't know, I really don't," Andy said seriously. "But if I hosted it, it would be a completely different kind of show."

"You could have Bob as a guest."

"I could have all my friends. You could be the writer in the last five minutes of the show."

"You could give the writers the first five minutes," I said.

"The writer always gets the last five minutes," Andy said. "But what would we talk about? I don't like girls' writing, all descriptions of what color things are. I like Hubert Selby, Jr. That's the kind of writing I love."

"You could say that," I said.

"You think that would work out?"

"Sure, then you could talk about it. Probably he'd call and volunteer to come on the show."

"That would be great! I'd love to have him as a guest. We could exchange different experiences we've had."

THE STUDENT greeters came in a van to pick us up. They still seemed bored. As we got near the university, Andy said, "I hear they have some big girls around here."

"What do you mean 'big'?" one of the students asked.

"Big. Tall."

"Some of the leaves are down already," I said. "I thought it was the height of the foliage season."

"It's been real windy," the student said.

"Every year there's some excuse for why it's not the way it's supposed to be," I said.

"The main thing is time," Bob said.

The sight of the state college gave me an idea of how the students had gotten to be so bored and depressed. It didn't look like any college I had ever seen but more like some factory buildings in a country behind the iron curtain. I imagined arriving at this college as a student without having ever visited. I knew I would have to turn around and leave, even if it was my one and only chance for a college education. I looked at the students and pictured their lives—day after day, looking at these buildings and going in and out of them.

"How long were you waiting for us?" Andy asked the students.

"About two hours," one said. "I have a psych exam today."

It was hard to believe that the student had any facts of psychology in his head.

"How much money will he take to give you a good mark on the test?" Andy asked.

"You have to bribe the prof," Bob explained.

"Ten, twenty, fifty, a hundred fifty?" Andy said. "How much, two-fifty? Bring him over here, we'll work it out."

"Money talks—we found that out today," I said.

"That's right, money talks," Andy said. "How do you think we got our eggs today?"

"The worst eggs ever," Bob said. "He figures, Okay, they wanna give me five dollars, I take the five and give them *eggs*!' "

"I know, I know," Andy said, laughing. "That thought occurred to me before they came."

"What did you think of *Animal House*?" asked the driver.

"I didn't like it," Andy said. "I was offered a part in it, but I didn't take it and I'm glad."

"What movies do you like?"

"What do I like? You mean now? Nothing. I don't like anything made now. There are some old movies I like. *City Lights,* by Charlie Chaplin. Wasn't it great? I don't like anything else Chaplin ever did. I don't think he was that good. Fellini's *8½. Miracle in Milan,* by De Sica. *The Phantom of Liberty,* by Buñuel. American movies— *Slaughterhouse-Five* and *The Graduate.* Those are my favorite things."

As we pulled up to the curb, a little old man was walking down the street ahead of us. "Wouldn't it be a good idea to drive up on the sidewalk and chase the guy down the street?" Bob asked.

"A great idea! If we had the time," Andy said.

"Here's the stage door," the driver said.

"I couldn't believe *Animal House*. It was nothing, right?" Andy said. "Okay, I'll tell you what I like. All the Frank Capra films. Like *Meet John Doe. It's a Wonderful Life.* Things like that."

Inside the auditorium, more bored-looking students were waiting around. They appeared to have just rolled out of bed after staying up all night drinking beer and watching TV. They all had long dark hair, and they were dressed in brown and black clothing. They introduced Andy to the musicians. It was a do-it-yourself introduction of shrugs and silence. "This guy has a test," one of them said about the drummer.

"Yeah, yeah, bribe the teacher," Andy said. "How much, five hundred bucks?"

"Nah, not this teacher," one of the students said.

"C'mon, c'mon—everyone has a price," Andy said. "Here, I'll write a check." He took a checkbook out of his pocket.

"Offer cash," Bob suggested. "A thousand in cash."

"Okay—one thousand in cash," Andy said.

"Tony Clifton won't be here tonight," Bob told me. "George thinks it's too hostile for colleges."

"Do you have brushes?" Andy asked the drummer.

"Not with me."

"I don't want anything fancy, you know," Andy explained to the band. "I'll be tap-dancing and playing the bongo drums."

"I only have time for one more song," said the drummer.

"We have four more songs to rehearse!" Andy said. "I'm trying to do it all by five."

"But my test is at five."

After the drummer left, Bob and Andy put one of their films into a projector. They were black-and-white musical shorts made in the 1940s. But Andy explained to the students that he had starred in the films, even though they must have known that his birthdate was 1949. "Here's a movie I did in Rio," he said.

"Which one are you?" the student asked.

"I'm the guy," he explained, pointing to a cowboy singing with some cowgirls. "In each one I'm a different character. In the next one I'm lip-synching. You'd never believe it was me."

"I didn't know you were that big. I know you're big, but . . ."

"It's shoulder pads. It took two and half hours for the makeup."

"The cowgirl's pretty cute."

"Oh, she was adorable. You should have seen what I did with her after the show."

"I know how those showgirls are," the student said.

"It's just what you think, too," Andy said.

"What are they wearing under the jackets?"

"Nothing. Here I'm the one in the black shirt." The cowboy was singing, " 'I've got spurs that jingle jangle jingle.' "

"Look, isn't that great?" Andy said. "I was lip-synching. I was so serious about it. It was a job, an educational film for schools, and they hired me as an actor."

"When was this?" the student asked.

"About ten years ago, in college. I answered an advertisement in the paper. I'm really proud of that shot."

"Educational in what respect?"

"I don't know. I don't understand why they made it. That's all fake—the mustache, hair . . ."

The cowgirls entered.

"She gave me a hard time," Andy said about the star cowgirl. "She was so hard to work with. I don't want to say in mixed company."

"How long did this take?"

"Two days, because of the problem with her. I don't want to say the word. Can I say it?" he asked. "Bitch, she was a bitch. Always complaining. 'The lights are too hot,' can't you tell? Now, this lady was funny. Off camera she was a barrel of laughs." Then the credits came on.

"What's the date? 1942?" Andy laughed. "We made it look like an old movie. We put a phony copyright on it."

AFTER THE concert was over Andy received fans outside his dressing room. His mother, sister, brother, and cousin had driven up to see the show. They came in and stood around while Andy talked to some of his fans. A white-faced young woman introduced herself as a transcendental meditator and they discussed their common meditation acquaintances.

WE DROVE in two cars to the diner. Somehow the meditator had gotten to be our driver. "I really should be in the car with my family," Andy said. "They came all the way up here to see me. Stop the car. I better go in with them."

"We're almost there," the meditator said.

"You don't understand, I belong with them," he told her.

In the restaurant, Andy's mother told me, over her dinner of diner eggs, that she had been Miss Schroon Lake during the 1940s. But she gave up her modeling career after marriage. For a while she helped her mother in the real estate business. "During one period, no one was renting any apartments and I had nothing to do, so I made a nutritional chart of my family's eating habits. I realized that none of them were getting enough protein."

BACK AT the motel room, Andy was kissing his relatives good-bye. The meditator was still hanging around.

"Does she plan to spend the night?" I asked Bob.

"Nah, he leaves them alone if they're from TM. It's something sacred."

"I promised her I'd wrestle her because she didn't get a chance in the show," Andy explained.

"I have to go to sleep," I said.

"Me too," Bob said.

"I don't know what I'm waiting around for," the meditator said.

"She was trying to save face, I guess," Bob said when we were outside.

THE NEXT day at noon, I looked out the window and saw Andy outside in his terry-cloth robe, standing at the meditator's car in the parking lot. He seemed to be giving her a kiss good-bye. "Hi," he called as he waved to me. "What's your name? I'll be right up."

. . .

WE HAD one minute to make a fifteen-mile drive to the airport. "I didn't meditate and I didn't have breakfast," Andy said when he opened his door.

"You have to make the plane," Bob said. "You'll have breakfast in Miami."

Two students arrived, still in their dulled state. They slouched outside on the van while Andy dashed around his room trying to get his belongings together. "Here!" he said as he threw me a beat-up canvas bag missing one handle. "Take my laundry. Look, you're carrying it wrong! Can't you see the handle will break off if you hold it that way? You can be so stupid sometimes."

"The plane must be taking off now," I said to Bob.

"Don't worry," he said. "We could make it."

"Where are my chocolate chip cookies?" Andy asked when we got into the van.

"Here," Bob said. "Will you look at him? Look what the guy eats for breakfast."

Andy had the box of cookies in his lap and was putting them into his mouth, one after another.

"They're delicious," he said. "Have one."

"Don't you feel that it's wrong to eat cookies for breakfast?" I said.

"Yeah, but I'm hungry."

"My room is full of fruit," I said.

"Her room is full of fruit! Why don't you come with us to Miami? I'll buy you a ticket. It'll be my treat."

"What for?"

"For fun! Aren't we having fun? Didn't you have fun with Bob and me?"

"I guess so."

"Really? See? Well, come with us. I used to think you were a pest when you were first trying to do your story, but now we've talked on the phone and hung out and you came to Albany and all and we ate in the diner and had breakfast in the motel, it's like we're friends—it's fun!"

"Well, I can't fly or I might go, to get the hour with you."

"She can't fly! Look how much fun she's missing out on being with us. Oh well, it's your mistake."

"She could be our mascot," Bob said.

"When you were in fifth grade, I was in seventh grade," I said.

"Yeah, Kawfman, we oughta show a little respect."

"Come on, what's more important, fun or respect?"

"When will you be in New York again?" I said.

"Why, are you going to ask me for more time?"

"Just the one hour."

"Why didn't you ask me last night?"

"Because you were with the meditator."

"I was willing to pass it up for you. You should have told me. Now I don't know what you're going to do."

"You said you had certain standards for women."

"She wasn't that bad."

"She didn't fit the description."

"Ah, they're all the same between the sheets," Andy said.

"Watch out, Kawfman—this is gonna be some feminist trap," Bob said.

"You know I don't mean it," Andy said to the students. "It's just a male-chauvinist character I like to play sometimes."

Bob wasn't surprised to hear that the plane was an hour late. He must have known all along, and the rushing was part of the act. "Good," Andy said. "We can have some breakfast."

He invited the students to come along, even though they'd already had lunch. "Come on, I'll buy everyone breakfast. No hard feelings about anything." The students agreed, but had to go back outside to move the van to a different parking spot. "I don't understand any of these kids," Andy said. "They don't seem enthusiastic at all about my being at their college."

"They do act pretty draggy," Bob said.

"Maybe they wanted Steve Martin and they couldn't get him. I'm going to wash my hands. Don't order without me."

"Last night I put the pillow over my head to block out the noise, and I dreamt that Andy was smothering me," I said when he'd gone.

"See?" Bob said. "I have those kinds of dreams all the time."

"UH-OH, WE have to order from the lunch menu," Andy said when he returned. "Can we get eggs?"

"Eggs aren't even good for you," I said.

"There's only an omelette on the lunch menu," the waitress said.

"Okay, should I get a plain omelette or a cheese omelette?"

"Plain," I said.

"Why plain?"

"Less fat."

"Okay, two large orange juices, both for me," Andy said. "Raisin Bran. A banana if you have any, bring it in the skin, not sliced. An omelette and some toast."

"Is it fresh orange juice?" I asked the waitress.

"No, concentrate," she said.

"Wherever we go, she has to ask about the juice," Andy said.

"She's like you," said Bob.

"But I keep it under control," I said.

"If you didn't, it could be a career, like with Andy," Bob said.

"Why don't you copy my act?" Andy asked me.

"I'm in a fight with a guy right now over that," Bob said.

"Yeah—Bob had a partner who used to throw up out of nervousness before they went on. Then Bob and he split up and Bob goes on with a ventriloquist's dummy and he has the dummy throw up. Do you blame the guy for being mad?"

"I thought it was a good idea, personally," Bob said with a shrug. They took their time over breakfast.

"We have a one-fifty plane," Bob reminded the waitress.

"But it's one forty-seven now," she said.

"Bob, this is your fault!" Andy yelled.

"My fault!"

"You knew when the plane was leaving!"

"You knew, too!"

"It's your responsibility to get me to places on time!"

"Let's make a run for it, not stand here arguing!"

"Look, there's the plane out there," said the waitress.

We ran down a staircase and through a long corridor. "You can't ever be on time!" Bob yelled. "You know it's your problem!"

"That's what I have you around for!"

"That's our plane," Andy told an airline employee, who had to signal the pilot out on the runway. Then he looked at Andy and Bob and shook his head in disbelief. Bob was running to the plane and Andy was clutching his bag of laundry and his box of cookies. His loden coat was flapping in the wind.

"Run with me to the plane," he said. "We can make a plan for our next meeting."

"Okay, if you promise you won't pull me onto it."

"Come on, Kawfman, you jerk!" Bob yelled from the doorway of the plane.

I ran out with Andy to the gangplank. He hugged me good-bye with his laundry and his box of cookies between us. "Keep in touch!" he called as he ran up the steps.

INTERVIEW WITH
A REPORTER

WHEN I DIDN'T hear from Andy by Christmas, I
called his mother to ask where he was. She told me that he
was in the hospital with hepatitis. "It's the type you get
from eating shellfish, the doctor says," she explained.

In January, Andy called to say thanks for the get-well
card from 1946.

"I thought you'd like it because the poem was so stupid," I said.

"I did! That's just the kind of thing I love," Andy said.
"All I did in the hospital was watch television," he said. "If
you'd called me when I was watching *Gilligan's Island*, I
would have been angry about the interruption and hung
right up. I realize that *Taxi* isn't so bad. There's a whole
other world out there of television even worse than *Taxi*.

People like you don't know about it. I really got into these programs when I was sick."

"*Taxi* is pretty bad."

"Did you see the one about the fat girl?"

"A few minutes of it. It was really bad."

"I thought it was touching. It was heartrending. I cried when I saw that."

"If you cried, it's because you're on the show."

"Come on! It was touching and heartbreaking. Why didn't you like it? Okay, okay. It really made me sick. You know how I feel when I'm on that set? Sometimes I just feel sick when I see the show. What am I going to do? I have a contract to be in it."

"When you first told me about it, you thought it wasn't that bad."

"Let's not talk about it. It makes me too sick. I'll call you in March when I come to New York."

WHEN I saw that Hubert Selby, Jr., had a new book out, I bought it and sent it to Andy in California. The next day I read in the *Times* that Andy was going to appear on *Saturday Night Live* that week. I bought another copy of the book to give him in person, even though I was embarrassed to ask for it both times.

I was waiting at the NBC reception desk for Andy when I saw him coming down the hall with a small teenage girl walking behind him. She looked like a fan, but she appeared to be with him. The fan followed him down the hall, along with a man dressed all in polyester—suit, shirt, and tie—all different plaids and stripes.

"Oh hi," Andy said to me, as if we'd never met. We all went into the dressing room and the man sat down in an easy chair. The fan leaned against the wall. "So you want to just interview me while I get ready?" Andy said to the man. I guessed that the man was a reporter.

"Here's your birthday present," I said, and I handed Andy the book.

"Oh, I bet I know what this is. Is it by my most favorite author? Is it his latest book?"

"Did someone already give it to you?"

"Yes, but I'm happy to have more than one."

"But I sent one to California, so now you have three."

"Look, it's all right. I'll have an East Coast copy and a West Coast copy. Did you read it? He's a great writer! He's in the same category along with Shakespeare and James Joyce."

"I don't think so," I said.

"Yes, the Oxford school did a thing on him and now

they consider him to be that. Oh look! An old card with a little poem. *Thanks!* She sends me all these old cards from bygone eras."

"Are you an Andy Kaufman fan?" the reporter asked.

"No, no, she's an author," Andy said. "She's been doing a story on me for a year. It took her a year because she hasn't gotten the one or two hours alone with me that she needs." He laughed.

"I've done three books," the reporter said, "and researching and writing a book is no fun, I know."

"This isn't a book—it's just a story, for a prestigious magazine," Andy said.

"Oh, Andy Kaufman, you're *hot* if they're doing you in profile!" the reporter said. "What do you think I should ask Andy?" he asked me.

"Ask him what you want to know about," I said.

"Well, Andy, I read a slightly flattering profile of you in—what was it?—*New West,*" the reporter said.

"What'd it say?"

"It was kinda 'We don't know if he has real talent'—wasn't that the drift?"

"Was it that one where she came to my apartment and we had ice cream? Was that negative? It was an East Coast magazine, right? No, that was flattering. The only time I wasn't flattered was a little thing in the *National Enquirer.*"

"Oh, I know," the reporter said. "In this article they were trying to expand you as a cult figure, and you can't do that—you either become one or you're not. I don't know whether I perceive you as that. Do you perceive yourself as that? I say to myself, Here's Andy Kaufman doing small clubs and *Saturday Night Live* and he finally saw the light."

"No, the reason I took *Taxi* was for a lot of reasons. The character of Foreign Man was a character I stopped doing, there's not much else I can do with Foreign Man. At first, people thought I was really like that and they'd get scared, they'd get embarrassed for me and all that. Then when they saw it was just an act, it wasn't brave anymore, and I always want to be new and brave. But people loved the character, so I decided to do it once a week on variety shows. You know how the character came from Caspiar, in the Mediterranean Sea, and while he was fishing the island sank so he came to the mainland and wanted to be in show business and he did clubs and shows and got on TV and now he's on *Taxi*. The background they wrote for him wasn't what I gave my Foreign Man. But I don't care. Then I go on shows and do new things I like to do."

"I don't know about you, Andy Kaufman—where you want to go in show business— But you're on a commercial show and not selling out your creativity?" the reporter said.

"No, because the money I make on the show I put into my concerts—I put all my money into that."

"The show's a hit now—are you gonna stay with it, are you gonna renew?"

"See, I believe the reason I'm in show business is to have fun, and wherever fun takes me, that's where I go. If I find something more fun, I do that. Whenever I have fun, that's where I go."

"No new deals have come to you from the show?" the reporter asked. "Is it too early?"

"I have a contract for next year."

"But, I mean, beyond that, *is your star rising*, Andy? *Are you going fast?* I don't want to compare you to Steve Martin, but, I mean, are you a hot property in show business?"

"Wait a minute. Let me explain. I'm not concerned about being a star. I don't care about ratings. I'm writing my third novel now. I've made a special for ABC which most people think is the most innovative special ever made—they compare it to Ernie Kovacs, who I've never seen—but the top executives at all the networks are against letting it be shown. So my manager said if I took *Taxi*, and was on TV once a week, I'd get a big enough name so the special would be shown. It's a wonderful thing and I'm very proud of it, I love it very much. That's why I'm doing *Taxi*, so I can do more of my own shows.

"The other thing I'm concerned with is my third novel, the Huey Williams story. I'd like to see a movie of it—an epic, like four hours, like *Ben-Hur*, that proportion, a mammoth biography—so everything I'm doing is headed towards that goal."

"What are your first books?"

"They aren't published," Andy said. "They were written more than ten years ago. I've been working on this one more than eight years. I don't want to publish the others, because I did one at sixteen and one at nineteen. I've outgrown them."

"So: the TV show is a fact of life in show business," the reporter said. "It's a means to an end. You can beat it, get on TV, get well known."

"Well, my manager knows my goal and he's doing whatever will get me to that goal faster, and he says this show will. Another goal of mine is to play Radio City Music Hall with the Rockettes."

"Well, what would you do—just walk out with them or what?"

"What would I do? Well, I do a two-hour concert now. I'm playing Carnegie Hall in April."

"Well, do we see segments on TV? Last time on *Saturday Night Live*, what was it you read—*War and Peace*?" the reporter asked with a smile.

"Yes, *The Great Gatsby*."

"Are these concert bits?" asked the reporter.

"That depends. Sometimes. I never know what I'm going to do until I do it actually that day. Sometimes I sing and dance."

"Do you feel like that now? It's time for rehearsal."

"Tonight there are these four musicians, and I'll probably come out and sing and dance while they play—I've always wanted to do that. If in my concerts, I feel, like if I've just read a good book, like when I finish this book chances are I'll wanna come out and read it. Like, I thought *The Great Gatsby* would make a good reading, but apparently it didn't, because I was asked to leave, they booed me off. I like to take chances, I like to do what I feel like doing, like if I feel tired I'll sleep, if I'm hungry I'll eat, if I feel energetic and happy I'll sing and dance."

"So we never see Andy Kaufman, do we?" the reporter said.

"Sometimes we do, like one time on TV I sang 'Oklahoma.' When I play the conga drums, that's me singing in a foreign language on *The Tonight Show*. Sometimes I talk like now."

"Everyone thought you were foreign," the reporter said, laughing.

"But I'd like to say, as far as the star thing goes, the goal is to play Radio City, to make that movie, get the special on the air. Another goal is this girl I was in love with in the seventh grade. I was too shy to meet her, have you heard? Because it's something I try to talk about so I can make contact."

"What's her name? We'll print it."

"I'm not gonna say, because she knows who she is."

"What school?"

"Great Neck Junior High. I realized I'd have to become famous and then I'd have the courage to talk to her. I don't feel I'm ready to say her name yet—*till* I've played Radio City, *till* I've got my special on—*then* and *only then* would I be worthy of her."

"Gee, that's great! Because so many people in show business, when people show up and say, 'Do you remember me?' You see a lot of that, don't you?"

"No."

"You will."

"I love it when my high school friends show up."

"I wonder if you'll stay as nice as you are," the reporter said.

"Who knows—maybe in ten years I'll be a bitter man," Andy said sincerely.

"One last question. What's Andy Kaufman really like?" the reporter said. "The one we saw reading—does he like to read? You're sort of a quiet fellow—you're not married, are you?"

"I've been married four times and I have eight kids. I love to say that."

"You're thirty now, are you?"

"I'll be forty-four in January."

"Ha-ha."

"I'd love for you to print that," Andy said.

"I have to laugh," said the reporter, "because that's how old I am. Forty-four. To you it's a joke."

"Look, I don't care about being a star. All I want is to get that girl, settle down, and marry her. Everything I've done for the past fifteen or seventeen years has just been so I can go out with the girl, not even marry her—just go out with her and hope things go well."

"Good—stay as nice as you are," the reporter said as he left. He was smiling.

As soon as the reporter was gone, Andy began muttering the interview questions to himself. " 'Are you hot?' " he asked himself a few times.

"Well, how was I? Now," he said to me, "I'm glad you witnessed this. Now you understand what I mean."

"You mean why you hate interviews? I always understood that."

"No, no! That you got the real story."

"Oh."

"That when I do interviews I have a pat story."

"But you told me that story, too."

"But you cracked it."

"I did? How can I tell?"

"You have to keep trying."

ANDY INTRODUCED me to the fan. Before I knew it, they were involved in a discussion of skin care. "This is what my doctor tells me—'Use Neutrogena with a buff pad,' " Andy said.

"My doctor is famous," the fan said. She named a famous dermatologist.

"Yeah, but my doctor just told me, 'Use Neutrogena,' " Andy said to the fan. "You have to decide who to listen to. Like me, I personally always use acid-balance soap, so to me Neutrogena is like, So I'll do it. It can't get any worse. See, I'm like you, I do all that stuff, I have bad skin."

"Why don't you just get some fresh air and sunlight?" I said.

"I sleep too late," Andy said.

"What about those 'Are you hot?' questions?" I asked.

"And how was my answer?"

"I think the more you say you don't care about being a star, the more he thinks you do."

"He does? How do you know?"

"If you said it after you were a star, he'd believe you. Now he doesn't."

"He thinks I'm a star now, doesn't he?"

"He can't decide."

"Why does he ask me if no matter what I say he's going to think something else?" Andy said sadly as he bent over his suitcase to unpack his costume for the rehearsal.

"If you said you wanted to be a star, he'd believe you. They never can believe anyone wouldn't want to be a star."

"Okay, so I told him—why do you say he doesn't believe me?"

"That's what these people are like."

"So what will he print? My quotes, right? No matter what he believes, he'll stick to the quotes. I should have said 'off the record.' Oh, I should have said, 'Yes, I'd love to be a star, but off the record I don't care.' My publicist is teaching me things to say and not to say. I need a publicist to tell people what I do at Carnegie Hall. Like in California, at Huntington Hartford, we did fantastic things and the public never knew."

"What things?"

"You didn't hear about it? One thing I did for my finale was a duet with Tony Clifton."

"How did you do that?" I asked, because I was under the impression that Andy did Tony Clifton.

"*Because, as I told you,*" Andy said, "*Tony Clifton is a real person.*"

"I meant, how did you coordinate it?"

"We rehearsed it together. 'Nothing could be finer than to be in Carolina in the morning.' Then I brought out the Rockettes and had them dance. Then I brought out the Mormon Tabernacle Choir, then Santa Claus, then we had snow fall from the ceiling, then I took the whole audience out to a restaurant, where we had milk and cookies, like I'm going to do at Carnegie Hall. Now do you believe me? You should, because it's true.

"Now, should I put gook on my hair or leave it? Do I have any more hair than last time? I'm really worried about it. I found out a way to get more hair even if you're bald. Three times a day you do this, I'm not kidding, I read it in a book, hand reflexology, same principal as foot re-flexology, every part of the hand corresponds to a point in the body, the nails are made from the same material as the hair, and you activate the nerves and grow hair. Rubbing the fingernails against each other like this, and you know something? I don't have time to do it. If I did, I'd be healthier."

"Do you have to sit and concentrate or just do it?"

"I don't know if you have to concentrate or can watch TV."

"I thought that reporter did okay. It took me months to get you to say what you told him."

"But you knew not to believe it was the real story. I tell every interviewer five things: the girl—Oh, I forgot to tell him I'm a busboy at the Posh Bagel."

"But you just told me about the girl, in Albany."

"That's because I didn't know about it before. One by one I've gotten things to talk about. I used to not know how to do interviews, but now I have it down to a science."

"You told me you met the girl."

"That was true. The false story is I'm still looking for her. I did meet her and go out, but we still didn't have that much in common. It made me feel good, like a celebrity. But what I want to do is hire an actress, she has to be a real opportunist, and I marry her and go on *The Tonight Show* and everyone's going to be heartwarmed by the idea, all America is going to be touched by it, and then it turns out she's a real opportunist bitch. Like, I'm talking to Johnny and she takes out a cigarette and interrupts me and says, 'Andy! Andy!'"

"I want to be the actress," the fan said.

"Well, we'll give you a chance to try out," Andy said. "Oh, I have to go. Will you two be all right together?"

Alone with the fan, I asked her if this was her first meeting with Andy. She said she was just a fan, he was letting her visit with him. She said she was seventeen.

"Do you know who you remind me of?" she asked. "You won't get insulted, will you?"

"I'm always prepared for the worst," I said.

"It's not bad, but people always get insulted no matter what. It's Goldie Hawn, the movie star."

"Andy has a fixation about her. Did he put you up to this?"

"No, but you never know what people think they're like."

"Who do you think you're like?"

"I like to think I look like Marie Osmond."

"You're much better-looking," I said, getting into the spirit of things even though I wasn't sure who Marie Osmond was.

"Thank you," she said happily. Then I left the dressing room and went to find Bob. He was standing out in the hall.

"Where's Andy?" he said frantically. "We gotta find him. I gotta talk to him!"

"Why—did something happen?"

"He's gonna ruin the whole spot tonight! He's gonna pull out a gun and shoot himself!"

"Oh," I said.

"Did that sound convincing?" Bob said on the way down the hall.

"YOU KNOW what I was thinking of doing?" Andy said when he saw Bob back in the dressing room.

"I was starting rumors in the hall," Bob said. "I said, 'He's lost his mind. He's gonna blow his brains out on TV.' "

"I'd love to do something like that," Andy said wistfully.

"You could say, 'I don't know how this got started. Zmuda's out of his mind. He used to write for me, then he flipped out.' Then I could say 'Andy meditated for six months and thought about it and he's gonna do it on TV.' "

Andy loved the idea. "You think Lorne would want me to go on to see whether I'm gonna do it?" he said.

"I think he would—even at the cost of blowing your head off onstage," Bob said.

"Sure, everybody would watch the show!" Andy said.

"Does he think that way?" I asked.

"He's a producer, isn't he?" said Bob.

"Most producers would say no," Andy said.

"Baaah—they got no sense of humor," Bob said.

"That's why they're producers," Andy said.

"Oh, let's see this—it's about Fred Silverman," Bob said as he looked at the rehearsal on the dressing room TV.

"Understand that this is the man that won't let my special get on the air on both networks, first ABC, now NBC," Andy said.

"It's always boring when they do Fred Silverman," I said.

"Now," Bob said, " 'When the men talk, the women shut up.' What is it, 'God, Man, Woman, Dog'?"

"Am I doing it right?" Andy asked, drawing lines in the air. "God, Man, Woman, Dog. Right?"

"No, do it again. God, man, woman, dog—woman/dog real close," Bob said.

"God, Man, Woman/dog. You know what? Save the rumors till I hijack the show."

"Why haven't you been on this show in so long?" I asked.

"He has to do *sitcom* in *Hollywood*," Bob said.

"What's that fan doing here tonight?" I asked.

"She asked me if she could come watch the show. Sooo . . ."

"I got it!" Bob said. "This writer here is doing a women's lib article, right? Turn off the tape," Bob said to me. "What did I say—did I say anything about women? We'll be assassinated!"

"We're both male chauvinists, right?" Andy asked.

"*You* are," I said. "You're a sexist."

"I am? I am and he's not?"

"You both are. You pretend you're not."

"Watch out," Andy said. "They have these hit commando groups, these feminists—these women's groups get squads together and get guys like us. I knew it from the start that she was out to get us. Come on, shut it off, you bitch. Let's pretend to break it now, then you can play it for people and they'll think we smashed it and beat you up."

"Now, after Carnegie Hall," Bob said, "you take the three thousand people—that's a lot, but maybe you could break them up into smaller groups. You could play the biggest practical joke on people ever in New York. You say, 'Now, folks, we're gonna go down to Seventh Avenue and everybody start screaming, "Godzilla! Godzilla!" ' "

"Ohhhh yes!" Andy said.

"It will be the biggest practical joke ever!"

"What if somebody has a heart attack?" I asked.

"Well, this could happen," Bob said. "This is a risk you have to take," Bob said.

"But couldn't I get arrested for inciting a riot?" Andy

said. "I know if you yell 'Fire' . . . but I don't know if you yell 'Godzilla.' " Andy said. He opened up his suitcase and started organizing his costume for the show.

"We could tame it down so it's commercially acceptable and agreed upon by the Police Department of New York City," Bob said. "I wouldn't want to do it otherwise. Are you kidding—I'm the producer of the show. They would take me away. They wouldn't blame you."

"Okay, now tell me about Plato's Retreat," Andy said. "Do you have to take your clothes off? I'm shy, I want my clothes on."

"Maybe for the first part you stay dressed, but for the other part I don't know," Bob said. "He doesn't want anyone to see his skin condition. Maybe he could wear a little shirt or something."

"You think I could?" Andy asked.

"I'm sure they have it worked out where it's very cool," Bob said. "You might just talk with a girl and go home."

"Who could I go with that would consent?"

"She'd go with you," Bob said. "Ha! Wouldn't that be a great way to end your story—you go with Kawfman to Plato's Retreat! That'd be funny."

"But, really, who do we know that would go?" Andy said.

"You could get a girl to go easily," Bob said.

"Who do we know?"

"You know what you do? You wouldn't even tell a girl," Bob said.

"Oh, that would be cruel," I said. "But you like to be cruel."

"I mean, a girl you know very well," Bob said. "Somebody who's not gonna freak out."

"Okay, but who?" Andy said.

"What would you do if Lorne comes up to you now and says, 'You're out of the show'?" Bob said all of a sudden.

"What would I do? Why, what would you do? What should I do? I'm getting paid. A free trip to New York. Plane fare. Hotel. Why should they do something like that?"

"It could happen."

"How?"

"I don't know—it could *never* happen! But what would you do?"

"What would I do?" Andy said as he kept unpacking. "I'd be a little sad. I'd feel a little rejected. A little sad. What's so funny about that? Why are you both laughing?"

CARNEGIE HALL,
APRIL 26, 1979

AFTER AN OPENING appearance by Tony Clifton, during which he sang the National Anthem while smoking a cigarette, the Love Family came out onstage to perform. The Love Family consisted of a large group of brothers and sisters in the age range of about five to fifteen. The Love Family started to sing some songs. One of the songs was "Aquarius," and another was "Climb Ev'ry Mountain." After the singing went on and on, the audience got restless and began to boo. A picture of Tony Clifton had been distributed to the audience, and printed on the picture was the suggestion to wrinkle up the photograph and throw it at Tony. Some people in the audience threw Tony's picture at the Love Family.

"I loved the Love Family," Mrs. Kaufman said when the subject came up after the show. "I wanted to take them home with me, they were so cute. Andy put them on because he thinks they're talented, not to be cruel. He doesn't have a cruel bone in his body."

"People threw things at the Love Family," Andy told me. "They thought I'd planned it."

"You knew people wouldn't like them," I said.

"People should like the Love Family. They're beautiful children."

"If they hadn't been on so long, it might have worked without the booing."

"I thought it wouldn't be too long because they were very powerful. There's the old show business adage: never follow animals or children."

"That doesn't go for a really bad act," I said.

"Wait a minute now! That act was very good. They happen to be fantastic! They're going to be big stars. It cost thousands of dollars to get them! I believe they're wonderful. They warm people's hearts. I believe people loved them until it went on too long."

"The audience liked it when it was so bad it was funny."

"Wait a minute, these kids are heartwarming! When they sing at the beach in California, everyone starts crying they're so touched by them. They say, 'Oh how cute.' Bob showed them to me and I liked them. They choked me up when they went out."

"The way the *Taxi* show choked you up with the fat girl story?"

"That choked me up. Yes."

"You forgot you admitted that show didn't choke you up, after you pretended that it did."

"I admitted it didn't? I thought it did. I think that I was fooling. I'm sure I got choked up. I remember almost crying when I saw that. I'm not kidding. Maybe I admitted it under the power of suggestion."

ANOTHER NEW thing that Andy did at Carnegie Hall was to bring out a white-haired actress and introduce her as the only surviving member of the cast that made the jingle-jangle movie he had shown in Albany, and which he showed again at Carnegie Hall. He said he would like to see her perform on the horse as she had done many years ago. She was given a child's toy, a horse's head on a stick. Andy told me later that he and Bob couldn't find the right prop, a half horse that the actress could fit into. "I got the horse at a toy store in Great Neck," he said.

The actress began to ride the toy horse as the orchestra played the song "I've Got Spurs That Jingle Jangle Jingle." Andy directed the orchestra to play faster, until no song could be recognized. He directed the actress to go faster to keep up. He ran over to the conductor, took the baton away from him, and began conducting the orchestra himself. The actress tried to keep up for a while and then she collapsed. Bob ran out onto the stage and called for a doctor from the audience. He said that this wasn't part of the act. A man came up onto the stage, said he was a doctor, and gave the actress some unconvincing cardiopulmonary resuscitation. The actress was covered up with a jacket. Then Andy returned wearing an Indian headdress and did a medicine dance and the actress got up. After an ovation, she walked off the stage and tripped and fell on the way.

"We were just thankful we got some old lady to come up on the stage and she went along with it," Andy explained to me a few days later. "How about when she died? Did you believe that? No? How about when they pounded her heart? How about when they covered her up with the jacket?"

"The Indian part didn't work."

"That's because *Bob* was supposed to hire *someone* to yell out after the lady died, *'That was in bad taste! What are you doing! You made my wife sick!'*, and I was waiting for someone to do it and no one did. I was supposed to start apologizing and then crying and then do the bongos. The Indian was not supposed to be good, it was supposed to be bad and provoke the outcry and booing."

"That would have been great," I said.

"Yeah, but a lot of things went wrong. We weren't even allowed to rehearse. Carnegie Hall is run by gangsters. In order to be let onstage, we had to hire these union guys and pay them a few hundred dollars, and then they refused to work. They sat around and played cards. The first time I saw the stage at Carnegie Hall was when I went on that night."

"How come I've never heard of this before?"

"Because people are afraid to talk about it. These guys are tough. They've taken over the whole city. That's why the TV industry has moved to California. They wouldn't even let us in the morning of the show."

"What have you been doing all these weeks since I saw you in March?"

"Preparing for the show. And lots of sex."

"Apart from that."

"That's all."

"I was just thinking about you, because there was a movie on about the doctor who discovered the cure for syphilis."

"Ohhh yes! But it looked boring to me. So, why didn't you come along on the buses we hired to Milk and Cookies?"

"I was afraid of what it might be."

"Well, there was a whole other show and you missed it. You missed out. And the next day I met a few hundred people at the Staten Island ferry and bought them all ice cream."

"What did you do at Milk and Cookies?"

"I re-wrestled the girl. Did you think she was a plant?"

"Yes. Why did she just happen to be wearing a leotard and slippers?"

"Do you think I'd be so stupid I'd have a plant dressed in a leotard and slippers? *Girls are doing this now!* She heard about the thousand-dollar offer and came prepared. And did you like the song I sang to the girl from seventh grade? The audience didn't hardly clap after that. They were really confused, or they just didn't like it? They didn't know if I was supposed to be funny or not?"

"I think they knew it was supposed to be funny."

"It's *not* supposed to be funny. What are you talking about! There was nothing funny about it! I was indulging myself in some serious country singing. I can sing the most boring song and they still laugh."

"I wish you had done the crying part."

"My manager hates that, the bombing and crying routine. He says to cut it short. I really get into it when I'm 'trying to be funny.' I say the stupidest things. That's when he says it's embarrassing and people walk out, but it's supposed to be embarrassing, I'm hoping to be bad and everyone is laughing and then I cry, because I say they're laughing at me, not with me. Did you like the way I had Robin Williams dressed up as my grandmother and sitting on the stage in the easy chair for the whole act?"

THE TWO HOURS

THE MOMENT HAD arrived for the two hours. "I can meet you for dinner, make a train back to Great Neck, and in between I have to meditate," Andy said.

"Do you want to meditate downtown at our house?" I asked.

"That might be helpful. If you wouldn't mind."

Andy didn't get downtown until after ten o'clock. I tried to get him to start meditating immediately, so we wouldn't be too late for any restaurant. I left him in the living room. While he meditated, I called some restaurants that might be open. When the hour was up, I noticed that my husband was in the bedroom watching *The Twilight Zone*.

"Better turn it off," I said. "He'll start watching and we'll never get out on time." But he had to see the ending, and when Andy came in, they watched it together, discussing plots from various episodes they had seen.

ONCE OUTSIDE on the street, in Greenwich Village, Andy looked around and said, "I used to be romantically in love with this place. I always wanted to be a beatnik, from the time I was in fifth grade. I wanted to be Maynard G. Krebs."

"Who is Maynard Krebs?"

"On *Dobie Gillis*. You never saw the TV show?"

"It looked bad. I gave up TV around that time."

"It was the greatest show! One of the best ever on TV! They never show it anymore except on 67, a station that can't afford any other shows. Oh, it was great! He's always sitting in the park under a statue called *The Thinker*. You know *Gilligan's Island*? No! Bob Denver. He was real dumb. A dumb beatnik. They'd say, 'Why don't you get a job?' and he'd say, 'Job?' 'Work?' It was a satire of a beatnik."

"Here we are—Spring Street Natural," I said.

"Oh, natural!"

"Is that okay?"

"Yes. Good. I had carrot juice today. Whenever I'm on the road and I see juice, I go in. Look, it's twelve on the button."

"Will they let us in?" I said.

"They may not."

"But they'll be nice to us anyway," I said.

"Make sure to tell them you called and they're expecting us."

They let us in and gave us the menu. Andy considered the number of choices. "So far I'm ordering artichoke hearts as an appetizer—salad, soup, scallops, vegetables, and brown rice," he said. "Is that too much?"

"Yes."

"What should I skip?"

"Skip the artichoke hearts. They're probably canned."

"Okay, I'll skip the artichoke hearts. Okay, so what do I have? Soup, salad—maybe I should skip the soup."

"Yes, skip the soup," I said.

"You think I'm ordering too much? I have to order dessert, too, in case the kitchen closes."

"Yes, it's too much."

"Okay. I'll have artichoke hearts anyway, even if they are canned I like them, and I'll skip the soup. Now is that still too much?"

"Don't worry about that."

"No? Then why don't I get all the other stuff, too, that I canceled?"

"We're out of tofu," the waitress said.

"Okay, what am I having? I canceled soup—maybe I should have soup."

"Yes, have soup," I said.

"Why? Maybe I should have what I'm having. Maybe I should have sautéed vegetables. Remember the days when—well, I used to be intimidated to go into a macrobiotic restaurant because of the people who work there. I used to be real nervous. I used to feel they were watching me and counting how many times I chewed my food. Fifty times for each mouthful—you know they count, and in order to work there you had to—oh—what did you order? That looks much better!"

"Brown rice."

"I wish I had ordered that," Andy said.

"You can have it. Here, take some."

"No, I have too much other stuff."

"Have this instead," I said.

"What are these on my plate?"

"Those are your vegetables."

"Oh. They don't look like vegetables."

"Now you have everything."

"Now I have everything."

"I think you have much too much."

"I have. I'm not gonna be able to eat this. She should take it back. Anyhow, Maynard G. Krebs. See, they were satirizing the popular opinion of beatniks. You know, lazy, good-for-nothing. And I used to want to be like him. So my parents took me to Greenwich Village when I was in fifth grade. They took me to Café Bizarre. I saw the advertisement—it said, 'Offbeat Place for Beatniks.' I thought, This must be where Maynard G. Krebs goes, even if he is a fictional character. Then, four years later, I went back there with my grandmother. When I first went, there were poetry readings and folk music, but later, with my grandmother—no more of that. But when I thought about it, I liked it even more. Gospel, calypso, African steel-drum bands—it was wonderful! That's when I started to get into conga drumming. That's how I was at fourteen. It's when I fell in love with the girl I'm searching for. You see, something within me woke up. Anyway, I wanted to be a beatnik. That was in '64."

"Wasn't beatnik passé by then?"

"Yeah, but I didn't know that. I was always a little bit behind. I was too young to be a beatnik. Finally, when I was old enough—well, I wasn't even old enough then—I was the only guy getting up in coffeehouses reading poetry when beatnik was all finished. I put on a fake beard and a beret—I had a Beatnik Kit, it was called. My uncle bought it for me. I only did that once. Usually I'd go without the Beatnik Kit."

"Were you serious?"

"Yeah, dead serious."

"What did people do when you read your poetry?"

"How should I know? I was so into it I didn't care. They'd clap politely—they were probably embarrassed, this kid reading this poetry. Then my parents wouldn't let me go to Greenwich Village—they made a deal with me I could go only once a month, and in the daytime. Then in high school a coffeehouse opened in the town near mine, called MacDougal East, and there were these Long Island housewives who'd been beatniks when they were young."

"That sounds so depressing."

"Well, you know, I was allowed to go there at night and read my poetry."

"Were there any beatniks left there?"

"Nah. It was mostly parents. There was a movie next door and they'd come out of the movie and go there. It was a store and the window was the stage, but it was fun for me—I'd read the poetry and play the bongos."

"The way you play them now?"

"No, I'd read my poetry and play the bongos at the same time."

"How did that go over?"

"I told you I don't know, because I wasn't sensitive to the audience then."

"What did you do at children's parties?"

"These are long stories. Should I go into them?"

"Unless it's too boring."

"It is, but I will if you want."

"Just tell about high school."

"Why? Because it's boring for you too, right?"

"No, because it's boring for you. I wish I knew how you got from being the person you were in your high school yearbook to who you are now."

"Why, because my hair was slicked down then?"

"No, because you looked as if you didn't know what was going on."

"It has to do with transcendental meditation."

"Do you look at that picture of yourself and say, 'Oh, what a jerk I was then'?"

"I was naive in a way, and I wasn't."

"Did you do what the normal kids did?"

"Oh no. I had special friends. We were into drugs before anyone else. We had long hair. Smoked grass. LSD. I didn't do that, though!"

"Taste this seaweed. Is seaweed supposed to taste like this?"

"That's seaweed."

"Is it supposed to taste like a Band-Aid?"

"Just fishy—that's what seaweed is. Very good for you. I

can't stand it! Now that you're talking about it—it never tasted good. But now—yuck! You have to face it. Anyhow, when I was seven, my grandfather gave me a sixteen-millimeter sound movie projector with sound movies and cartoons. My father would show them as a treat—the whole family would gather round to see them. We had Abbott and Costello, horror films, *The Mummy*. So one day I ran the movie projector, and that meant we didn't have to be dependent on my father. Then Aunt Inger said, 'Want to run the movie projector at Barbara's birthday party?' I was seven, and all the other kids were eight. And word got round, and before I knew it I was asked to run the projector at other birthday parties, and they paid me for my services—they'd buy me a toy."

"What made them want you to do it? Was there some special way you did it?"

"*You're the first person who ever asked me these questions and they are so stupid I can't believe it! I was asked to run it at Aunt Inger's and then all the others asked because it was enjoyable, okay?* Now. Listen to this—James Brown. My friends and I were the first to be into black soul stuff like this. And if my memory does not fail, we were into the Rolling Stones before anyone else, too. Guess what. I'm not going to eat this dessert. We'll go somewhere else for ice cream. Your husband—I didn't remember him looking

like that. Last year a writer interviewed me for a magazine
and I got her husband confused with your husband. Now,
yours is a very nice guy. He's very level-headed, a nice, lik-
able man, a good man. I respect him. He's a 'good man for
you.' Anyway, when I was fourteen, I put an ad in the
paper and I started being hired out to strangers' houses. In
other words, I was a professional. I'd show movies, do
magic, play games, pin the tail—no, pin the nose on the
clown, play guitar, I'd do things with the tape recorder."

"Did anyone call it comedy?"

"Of course not! It wasn't comedy. It was just playing
with kids."

"When did it get to be called comedy?"

"In college, when I did nightclubs."

"You know the part in your act where you explain that
you went away to college in Boston and you realized you
were Jewish and you went home at Passover and read
prayers in a Jewish accent? It sounds like something a regular comedian would tell."

"I know, it falls flat. There's no reason for the sentences
except that it really happened and I want to say the whole
thing in a Jackie Mason Jewish accent. Because when I
discovered I was Jewish, I went around talking in a Jewish
accent. *Un-der-stand?*"

"What does Bob think?"

"Bob? Bob? You know what else I don't like? These vegetables aren't cooked right. They're hard."

"That's the idea."

"I know, I know. I steam my own vegetables, but I get them soft—that way they're easier to eat. They're all cold now anyway. Who needs it? I can't eat another bite. Watch your machine that it doesn't go off."

"It tapes a whole hour."

"We've been here an hour. Here. Let me check it. Listen, honey, you have very few minutes left. It's going to stop any minute. Then you're going to turn it over, right?"

"I don't think that the subject runs the tape."

"I taught you the whole thing—you even got my tape recorder I told you about! But you should have gotten the cover for it. They said to me, 'What extra do you want?' and I said, 'Phone jack,' and they said, 'You want a cover?' and I said, 'What for?' and they said, 'To keep it clean,' and I said, 'Ehhhh,' and they said, 'Look, these things are at a premium—people wait months for them, but we have them in now, so you better get it,' and I said, 'Okay!' Two dollars extra. How much did you pay for your machine? One-forty-five? That's what I paid for mine."

"First they told me one-sixty-five," I said. "And then I told them I saw it elsewhere for one-fifty, so then they said okay, one-forty-five. But you could probably tell them one-forty, and they'd say okay, one-thirty-five. Who is that zombie voice you and Bob are always doing with each other?"

"Norman. We can't say who it is. He's a paranoid schizophrenic, and if he finds out we're doing him, he'll come and kill us. Bob is the one who really does Norman. Bob won't let me imitate him. Bob does him better than anybody—that's Bob's thing, and he doesn't want anybody to think I created the character. He's right, because it's his character and it's a real good character. He's more business-oriented than I am, for his own career, which he wants to have."

"As a what?"

"As a what? He's a great actor, writer, and director."

"He wants to do everything?"

"Write, direct, and act, just like I want to do that, too."

"Just like everybody."

"Yeah. But not just like everybody. Because they wanna do it for their ego, and I want to do it just to find that girl."

"Why does Bob want to?"

"Because he's a great artist—he wants to do something great for the world. Oh, I know! I'll eat the strawberry off the cake. Then we can go get ice cream."

As soon as we were out on the street, Andy hailed a cab. "But we're only ten blocks away," I said.

"But we took a cab here."

"That's because we were late."

"Well, we hailed it, so we have to take it. I'm sorry—I didn't realize where we were. Anyhow, I want to cover some more points. There are five main points I say to every interviewer specifically so that there will be enough pressure from the public to get the networks to show my special. They say it's too far out for the American public. Anyhow, then there's my third novel, and three: there's The Girl, and then there's my wrestling of a girl in my act. I challenge any woman in the country to pin me down to the count of three—she'll win five hundred in cash, and as time goes on, the money will get more and more."

"I don't get the wrestling," I said.

"I know, no one does. My manager hates it, too. Anyhow, then four: every Monday night I work as a busboy at the Posh Bagel simply because I like the work. Another thing I'm telling people is—you know I'm telling you which is and which isn't true—but you, I'd appreciate if you don't tell. Let's get out here and walk."

"The things I really want to know, you won't tell me," I said when we were out in the street.

"Like what?"

"Like how you went from being a jerk to what you are now."

"Okay. A jerk. The year after high school, everyone went to college and I didn't. I drove a taxi and trucks. I drank heavily."

"Were you very unhappy?"

"I was unhappy most of the childhood. I had no confidence. I was shy with girls in general."

"What did you think would become of you?"

"I thought I'd be a truck driver. I thought I'd found my vocation. Then one day I decided to become a businessman. This is really something. I don't think we should walk around here at night. So one day I was tired of driving trucks."

"What did your parents think?"

"My father said, 'Andy, you have so much more you can do. You're wasting your life.' The first day after high school, he said, 'I want you to get a job,' so he was glad I got a job, but then he saw I was just staying there driving a truck."

"Didn't they want you to go to college?"

"They understood it might not be right for me. They understood that. But my father said, 'You could do more with your life. You used to perform at children's parties. You could do something with that.' So I decided to become a businessman. That lasted a week or two. I quit driving the truck and was a businessman. I'd dress up every day in a suit and tie and I'd walk the streets every afternoon and I'd had these cards printed up—they said, 'Andy Kaufman, Businessman,' and I'd walk the streets and I wouldn't even give them to anyone."

"In New York City?"

"No, in Great Neck. I'd walk the streets as a businessman, and I decided I wasn't getting anywhere. I was a failure as a businessman. I wasn't making any money."

"What business was it?"

"Just business."

"Is that a true story?"

"Now, can I tell you the truth about that? The truth is that I decided my children's-party-entertainment work was a lot more easy work and a lot better business than driving trucks. I'd perform an hour and make fifteen to twenty dollars, and that was a lot more profitable than seventy-five a week, ten hours a day, six days a week. Much better! So I had pamphlets printed up—'Uncle Andy's Fun House.' And I put ads in the paper and went into business again the way I was in high school, so I'd be working two to three parties a day and making a week's truck salary in one day. But it didn't work that way, so what I tell people now is—I haven't told any interviewers this yet; I just realized it would make a good story—dressing up as a businessman. I should say it. But I did consider the parties business, I was in my own business. And then my friend said, 'You should go on TV and become a children's clown like Bozo!' So I put it together—I should go on TV as a clown and continue my party-entertainment business and get such a name that I'd have the biggest children's-party-entertainment business in the world and franchise it and train people.

"So I went to this junior college that anyone could get into—it was all kids who were trying to keep out of the Vietnam War, not a real college. So, you see, it was so cold in Boston that I'd dress up in a shirt, a sweatshirt, a sweater, a jacket, a coat, raincoat. Much like I dress now, but more so. And of course I've always been late for every-thing, so I'd be late for class. So I'd come in late and I would just take off my layers of clothes one at a time and throw them on the floor—I'd stand there, I'd been run-ning because I was late, so I'd be panting, and I'd try not to be conspicuous, and people would watch me. After a few minutes, the whole class would be laughing—it would be disrupted completely.

"The teacher was a nice guy—he'd laugh, too. Of course he didn't like that I was always late. But he told me at the end of the semester to go into TV. 'Don't stay in radio, because you're very visual.' I said, 'I'd like to be in TV, so I thought I'd major in radio, so I could be a great disc jockey and work my way into TV.' He said, 'You know, Andy, if you want to be on TV, major in TV.' I said, 'Yeah!'

"I'm very grateful to this man. I felt he taught me a great lesson: If you want to do something, do it, don't beat around the bush."

"You're still doing that now. You're in a sitcom so you can be famous, so you can get your special on, so you can make movies."

"Ohhhh! Right! No, I don't have a choice now. It was easy then—major in radio or TV. Now it's different. So I majored in TV and started performing in front of grown-ups for the first time. They'd give out assignments, like the song 'MacArthur Park.' You've seen the way I do it with the Yiddish accent, overemotional—that's a true story. Then we had an assignment to do an hour's TV show. So I did Uncle Andy's Fun House."

"Did they think that was comedy?"

"No, they thought I was nuts. They would laugh at me."

"Weren't you trying to be funny?"

"No. I realized that all my life I'd been laughed at, and I used to not like it, and that's why I was so unhappy, and then I realized, when I started meditating, that, Wait a minute, being laughed at is fine. So I started using it. Not being laughed with, being laughed at. One day, I looked in the mirror and it was summer vacation, I had my hair parted in the middle and I had a mustache and I looked like an old-time comedian, and I realized for the first time, Andy, you can be a funny man if you really want to. All my life I'd been such a serious guy and never could tell a joke, never be the life of the party, and so I looked at myself in the mirror and said, 'Andy, you can be a famous funny man if you would like.' "

"And what did you say back to yourself?"

"I said, 'Oooookay!' "

ICE CREAM

I'D LIKE SOME chocolate chocolate chip ice cream and some hot chocolate," Andy said to the waitress at our next stop.

"Whipped cream?"

"Oh yes, even some extra cream."

"Extra whipped cream?" she asked. "Is that what you meant?"

"I really meant cream—whipped cream or cream, it doesn't matter. I just like to put more in so it gets cold."

"I don't think it's real whipped cream," I said. "It's sprayed from a can."

"Who cares? So. I don't know how deep you want me to get into this."

"As deep as you can stand to."

"Oh no. It's just so tiring. There's so much to cover. There's my whole life story."

"How do you think I feel having to get your whole life story in two hours after trying for a year?"

"Why didn't you just ask me?"

THE LAST HOUR AND THE
FOREIGN MAN

"I WAS NEVER funny. What I found out in college was that when I was the most serious was when people were laughing."

"So you just kept it up and people would laugh?"

"Yeah! Then, one day in college, these black guys were having a 'Soul Time' show and asked me to be in on it. They said, 'We want you to be the comedy relief.' Now, I had never done comedy, but they were laughing at me all the time on the street—I was their buffoon. So I decided, 'I'll imitate Elvis Presley and play the conga drums,' and that's what I did.

"Then I saw an ad in the paper from a girls' school down the street—they wanted acts, so I said, 'I'm not an act, but I have a novel—I've been reading it to friends in travels all over the country.'

"So they set it up for me to go to their dorm and give a formal reading. They loved it, and it was reviewed. Then she said, 'How'd you like to do a half hour of comedy?' I said, 'I've never done comedy—I don't know how. All I know how to do is imitate Elvis and play the conga drums.' She said, 'Andy, I'm sure you can put something together.' So I put a lot of thought into it. And this girl, who was seventeen and coming to see me when I was twenty-one—I would sing these songs to her on the guitar—'That's Amore,' 'Strangers in the Night.' You know—all those dumb songs from another generation. And I said to my friends, 'I'm gonna perform in a coffeehouse—imitate Elvis, play conga drums, sing "That's Amore," ' and they all laughed. Just doing Elvis in a coffeehouse was ludicrous. People thought I was serious—they'd look at me and say, 'Am I dreaming? Is he for real?' There—I wasn't trying to do comedy, just doing what I did, and they loved it. So I was asked back, and I came back with 'Mighty Mouse.' It was a song I'd been doing in my room for years, fantasizing doing it on a children's TV show. And it worked! I thought they'd go, 'What is this guy doing?' but they clapped for it, they laughed for it, they thought I was a comedian. I said to myself, 'Well, I'm just gonna continue doing what I'm doing.'

"When I wanted a job in a real theater, they'd say, 'What do you do?' and I'd say, 'It's hard to explain.' They'd say, 'Forget it!'

"Then, Foreign Man. One of those afternoons when I'd read my poetry and played the congas at the Café Wha?— I was fourteen—everyone in the place was so embarrassed by this other man there with this sort of Pakistani accent trying to do these terrible jokes. God, they were so bad— anecdotal jokes—and then he'd say, meekly and shyly, 'Vell, dat ees my story,' and no one would laugh, and then he'd say, 'Vell, dat ees all I vented to say,' and still no laughter or applause—just dead silence and painful embarrassment, and then he'd say, 'Vell, tenk you vedy much.' My friend and I were hysterical. You know, quietly hysterical. When we got outside, we went crazy.

"So in college I saw that the audience wouldn't accept it if I started out with Elvis Presley. They were offended. They'd go, 'What—he thinks he's handsome or something?' I decided that my natural innocence—I'd lost it after the first few times I did my act. Like with 'Mighty Mouse' I was genuinely innocent—I thought I could get back to being more innocent as the Foreign Man. Maybe I could get famous as a guy who speaks foreign and the only thing he does is Elvis Presley. So the first time I tried it, in a little coffeehouse in Long Island right down the block—a wine and cheese shop—the whole act was Foreign Man, and when I got to the Elvis part, I said, 'So now I vould like to do de Elvis Presley.' Then I decided it was very strained doing the whole act as Foreign Man. See, when I auditioned at the Improvisation and the Bitter End as myself doing Elvis and playing the conga drums, it didn't work and I didn't make it. So when I did Foreign Man in Long Island, I could see that I was on the right track. I auditioned in Long Island, and the guy said, 'I'll give you a chance.' So I became friends with the guy, because I got a standing ovation that night. I did Foreign Man, Elvis Presley, and myself, and it worked great.

"A couple of years later, the guy told me the reason he put me on was because I was so crazy—not a good act—he didn't know I had such stage presence. So I acquired a following there. Every Monday, I was on every time, and not paid, and I tried again at the Improvisation and made it.

"The rest is history. I met Bob, and we'd share ideas—he's the only guy who thought like me. So I said, 'If I ever have my own show, you can write for me.' But before I'd ever met him, I'd had the idea I'd take a gun out onstage and blow my brains out. I was seeing a psychiatrist since age three."

"Have you ever seen a good one?"

"How should I know? How can you write this? You don't know anything juicy about me. You don't know about the craziness, the insanity. You don't know the half of it."

OUT IN the street, some unsavory-looking youths came toward us. "I don't feel we're safe, because when I'm alone they leave me be because I pretend I'm crazy," Andy said. "But I'm so crazy, no girl would be with me. So with you here, it doesn't work.

"Anyway, with a regular interviewer, I know where they're going, so I give them what they want, like the *Enquirer*—they want to hear about girls and sex. If I was a writer, knowing what I know about me, I'd make it up. I'd use my time with Andy Kaufman to write a fictional piece, but I'd say it was true. Not lies like the *Enquirer*, but it would be surrealistic. But I shouldn't tell you. You have the vision."

"THE REASON I'm into getting all these girls now is because it's psychologically rewarding. These are the desires I've always had, I feel like I want to fulfill them."

"But most of these girls are so empty-headed."

"It started in California when I retired from show business for six months. I saw all these girls on the beach. You know that six-foot girl I was trying to get the other night? Well, I've always wanted a six-foot girl. When she left, I called this other girl who is such a sweet, wonderful darling—she's not sexy, you know, she's too short. For instance this weekend I may have a tall sexy girl and the short nice girl, too, and I'm looking forward to both. Look, I like lust and then I like love. One time at the Posh Bagel, there were these two girls there and they were enticing me to come over—putting their hands on my leg, and after work they kind of seduced me into inviting them over to my house to wrestle—and we all took our clothes off to wrestle and of course it turned into sort of an orgy—it was fun."

"It doesn't sound like fun."

"It's a man's fantasy! But you know something, I couldn't even get into it, because it was all lust and no love. And plus, they weren't that pretty. I couldn't get involved. It's a man's fantasy, but one girl was on the fat side and the other didn't shave her legs. That's the new thing now with feminists. That's when it all started, with women's liberation. Let's face it—women should shave their legs. Anyway, you should read Hubert Selby, Jr. I know you say you hate his writing. You remind me of my high school librarian—when I told her I liked him, she said, 'Oh, Andy, I'm surprised at you!' It's poetry—each word is a masterpiece. He takes years to write each book—I think he does—it doesn't matter if he does or not."

"Isn't there any other writer you like?"

"He's the only one. If you want to read my favorite book, read *The Demon. Last Exit to Brooklyn* is considered a masterpiece, but *The Demon*—he outdid himself. Also *The Room*—I didn't like it, because it's all staged in one place, the room, but you might like it literally. It all takes place in a man's mind. You know who used to be my favorite author? Kerouac. *On the Road* was my favorite book. *The Town and the City* was great. Real boring for the first three hundred pages, but the last two hundred make up for it."

"Remember when the reporter suggested you were a serious guy who liked to read a good book? Maybe he was right."

"I never read except before bed."

"I mean about being serious. Maybe you have no sense of humor."

"Yeah, I have absolutely no sense of humor."

"It took me all this time to figure it out."

"How about with Bob—I have some humor then. Anyhow. So read *The Demon*. That's my mind in a nutshell. That's me. That's what would happen if I didn't have self-control, and Bob would be like that, too. As a matter of fact, every man would be, too. There's a demon inside of every man, and that's what would happen if man let the demon get the best of him.

"I've led a peaceful kind of life at times, and yet I've still had that demon inside me. *The Demon*. I love that book! I was flipping out as I was reading it. I was screaming with delight! What I suggest to you is, read it. Sure, the guy talks like a dummy, but that's because the main character talks like that, so people don't understand—they think he's just a dumb writer. I heard from someone who knows him that he has a good sense of humor. How come you're not put off by Dostoyevsky?"

"Have you ever read *Crime and Punishment*?"

"No, the print's too small. It would take years and years to read it. Okay. If you were to read Selby, in your case I would recommend not reading *Last Exit to Brooklyn*.

Maybe I'll recommend you to read his new book when I finish it. It's about a boy and his mother."

"You should read *A Mother's Kisses*, by Bruce Jay Friedman. It's about a boy and his mother."

"Look, just by the fact that you're disgusted by Selby points out what a good writer he is. You can't get disgusted by words on a page unless it's so great. I like horror movies. I like to be scared. I like the whole spectrum of emotions. I like to laugh, I like to cry. I don't think any sense of humor is funny. Rarely. Jean Shepherd is funny."

"You're just lucky you're not like any of the people you admire."

"Granted you may think he may not be a nice man. You may think his personality is stupid, he's really boring doing certain things, but he has a talent as a storyteller."

"What about the other people you admire, like Steve Allen?"

"Steve Allen? A wonderful host. Fifteen or seventeen years ago his show was wonderful and a big influence on me."

"When you name the other people who have influenced you, nobody knows what you're talking about."

"Who? I say Steve Allen, Hubert Selby, Buddy Rogers, and Elvis Presley. Who could it be? You know what I should say from now on in interviews? I should say Merv Griffin or Mike Douglas. Something like that. Wouldn't it be ludicrous? Did you like the way I had Robin Williams dressed up as my grandmother and sitting on the stage in the easy chair for the whole act at Carnegie Hall?"

"Yes, even if it wasn't Robin Williams."

"Trust me. It was Robin Williams. I'd tell you if it wasn't. Why do people not believe me?"

IN THE JAGUAR WITH
ANDY'S MOTHER

ANDY'S MOTHER AGREED to meet me when she was in the city. A complicated plan was worked out. She was driving to New York with Andy's grandmother, Mr. Kaufman's mother, in order to drop her off at the apartment of the other grandmother, her mother. Then she and I would sit downstairs in her car, a brown Jaguar, because there were no legal parking spots.

Outside the apartment house Mrs. Kaufman introduced me to the first grandmother and said, "She's writing a story about Andy." The grandmother looked like a real grandmother. She had white hair and pink cheeks and was smiling.

"I've been working on the story for a year," I said.

The grandmother smiled more and said, "With him you need a year."

"What do you think about Andy's big success?" I asked her.

"I'm more surprised than anything else," she said. She was still smiling.

INSIDE THE Jaguar with Andy's mother, I asked her if she'd noticed anything unusual about him when he was a baby.

"Oh, he was quite unusual. At nine months of age, he used to pull himself up in his crib. And next to his crib was a dresser with a little Victrola and we used to buy children's records, and he couldn't turn it on and off, but he could pull the plug out and put it back, so we kept it on all the time and he'd use the plug to put it off or on. He put the records on himself—he knew from the labels which records had which songs. He was unbelievable. Just before his second Christmas, my folks bought him a little white wagon with a Victrola on it. He had a record collection. He did the same with books."

"Did you think he must be pretty smart?"

"No, I didn't think anything. I just thought he liked records."

"Did you notice anything else when he was a baby?"

"He was always a loner. He was great with adults, but he was shy with kids his age. He was two when Michael was born, and then he would just stand and look out the window. It was a little heartbreaking."

Andy had told me I could ask his mother anything. "She'll tell you. She told me that when I was two I stared out the window like a depressed old man."

"I had some peculiar ideas with Andy," Mrs. Kaufman said. "Well, when I was pregnant with Michael, I had lost my regular help. She became pregnant. But she didn't have a husband. And I was in bad shape, because I was in bed seven months with Andy and with Michael for three months and I was kind of sick, and it wasn't easy. I used to pass out. I put a little note in Andy's pocket—if anything happened to me, this is who he is and to call his father. It was tough taking care of him. My mother-in-law said to me, 'You know what I used to do with my son Jack—he was a wild one,' and Andy was wild, he was so cute, but he was rough, he had a temper, he never turned blue, he turned black. One time, he ran out the door—no pants— and he was down the block before anyone could get him. He was always a fast runner. So my mother-in-law said, 'Tie him up with a rope,' and I tied him up with a rope, tied him to a tree out front, and I took one look at him and he looked like a wild animal. And I couldn't stand it. I called the doctor—a new pediatrician, because the old one didn't seem to be able to help me with anything—and he said, 'Don't you ever tie a child up.' Yes, he could get all over the place. But it was terrible. From that time on, Andy was pretty good with the doctor. He'd had a lot of psychology in his background.

"I had the strange idea that children are always supposed to be happy and smiling. So when Andy was four, I said, 'He just doesn't smile,' because when he was a baby I used to hold him in my arms and sing to him and he used to laugh, he used to have such a great time, I guess until Michael was born. When he was the only one. Nah, it was before that. When I was pregnant, I just didn't have the time for him. I was sick in bed, grumpy and grouchy. So when he was four, I took him to New York to a psychologist and he sent him to have him tested and they said they felt Andy could use some play therapy. So we took him to someone in Long Island who gave him play therapy, but when summertime came and she wanted to go on her vacation, she said, 'He doesn't need any therapy anymore. He can go to summer camp.' So he went to summer camp. He probably didn't want to. He was all right at camp, but when he started school he was a real loner—I understand from his teachers he was bored. The school kept saying that he was a problem. And we were too dumb to fight, so we accepted it. We sent him for more counseling. We should have fought for other things. He should have been put ahead in school and not expected to do the ordinary, normal things. A special school—for what it cost for psychiatry, it could have been done. Andy was always performing. I never knew about professional schools. But I never even thought of Andy going into any profession anyway. But he could have used a special school, for gifted children. I didn't think of it. And neither did anybody else. The psychologists at school, they just called him a problem. He was having problems and he was unhappy. He went to psychologists and doctors until he was in college and found meditation. Meditation was so fantastic, what it did for him, that I had to go. And some of my friends had to go, too. He was always an angry person, unhappy and impatient. It calmed him down. It made him aware of himself and other people. He was able to accept people's shortcomings and laugh about them. Before that, he and his father didn't see eye to eye on things. He smoked a great deal, he drank wine, beer, smoked pot. For us it didn't seem right. We were still dragging him to a—well, not dragging him, he wanted to go, to help himself—to a psychiatrist. But from the time he started meditating, he never took another puff or a drink. If I make a dish at home with any liquor in it, he doesn't eat it. He had a lot of psychiatry, and I did, too, because he went to the kind of place that believes if a person needs help, that's only one person—the family needs to go. I was just going for Andy and all I did was say what was on my mind, but nobody was helping me. In his senior year, they were going to leave Andy back. His College Boards were great, but his grades were terrible and he cut classes all the time. His English teacher wanted to flunk him and keep him back because . . . Well, just because. The warden and the English teacher came together. They were new, from the Middle West. Whenever we went to talk to them, we felt like we were sitting in a prison.

"When we took Andy up to college he was in the back of the car with a carton of cigarettes and a six-pack of beer. We were making him promise, 'You have to be good. You can't smoke pot—they'll throw you out,' and he said, Okay, okay, okay. The year before, when he stayed home and was just driving a truck and taxi, it wasn't what he was doing that was the bad part—it was that he was so unhappy and angry. So at the end of the year, Mr. Kaufman told him that he owed him an education and he should go get it then or he never would. So Andy got hold of some advisory committee and sent away to millions of colleges, and then where does he apply? To one that's not even on the list. Not that he was accepted at Harvard or Yale, but there were some good colleges. He wanted to go to Graham Junior College and that was it. We were just delighted he was going. I had decided I expected nothing of him, so I was thrilled when he'd have a good day."

"What happened when he started to do really well?"

"Oh, he didn't do really well until just recently. He didn't get much encouragement from us. All the times he was knocking his brains out working for nothing, we'd say, 'You're putting in so much time, why don't you get money for it?' and he'd say, 'No, I have to be seen, get exposure, that's what matters.' He fought the two of us. He lived at home, he got no money from us, he worked as a waiter, did odd jobs."

"What did you think he should be doing?"

"Well, we didn't know he was going to be this kind of a star. My feeling was, you know, maybe he wants to go on Channel Thirteen with a little kiddie program. I thought he'd be a children's entertainer. When he did the children's parties, he was given fifty cents once, and once a little gift. Then, when he was twelve, he put an ad in the paper and said he'd do the party for five dollars. But for five dollars he threw the whole party—he bought the favors and everything. Like at Carnegie Hall, giving the milk and cookies to the whole audience."

"When did you get an inkling that he'd be a big success?"

"You know, I can't tell you. The whole thing seems like

a dream. The best part is that he's happy. When I used to drive him to the psychiatrist when he was twelve, thirteen, I'd say, 'What you do in life has to be what you love. Wake up every day and say, "I can't wait to get to work." ' And now he has that. It's a dream come true."

In 1984, Andy Kaufman died of a rare kind of lung cancer. He was thirty-five years old.

Acknowledgments

The author wishes to thank the John Simon Guggenheim
Foundation for supporting her work.